BUILDINGS FACE THE FUTURE
IS THERE PERHAPS MORE TO ARCHITECTURE THAN YOU THINK?

BY
DIANA ROWNTREE

ARCHITYPE

First published in 1994 by ARCHITYPE
19 Front Street, Corbridge
Northumberland NE45 5AP

with the assistance of The Building Centre Trust

© Diana Rowntree
All rights reserved

Typeset by the AA Print Studio

Printed by E. G. Bond Limited

British Library Cataloguing-in-Publication Data

ISBN 0 9521705 0 7

CONTENTS

		Illustrations	6
		Acknowledgments	7
	Chapter 1	The Muddle We Find Ourselves In	8

WHAT ARE BUILDINGS FOR?

Chapter 2	Our Containers	12
Chapter 3	The Business of Building	21
Chapter 4	The Art of Architecture	26
Chapter 5	The Play of Masses Brought Together in Light	38

WHO ARE BUILDINGS FOR?

Chapter 6	Who Are Buildings For?	44
Chapter 7	Vernacular	48

KEEPING UP WITH LIFE

Chapter 8	Planning for Change	56
Chapter 9	The Demands of Freedom	65

WHAT ARE ARCHITECTS FOR?

Chapter 10	The General	70
Chapter 11	The Gap	73
Chapter 12	Architect and Client	76

WHOSE RESPONSIBILITY?

Chapter 13	Of One Mind	84
Chapter 14	For Better or Worse?	92
	Photographers' credits	102
	Index	103

COUTANCES CATHEDRAL FRANCE
Contemporary with Chartres and Amiens

The building as we see it today was built after the fire of 1218 AD. The tree-like masonry brings the huge loads from the vaults safely to earth, via the ribs and columns.

STUTTGART AIRPORT
GERMANY 1992
Architects: von Gerkan & Marg,
Hamburg

Steel trees have their own grace. They occupy less space than their stone forebears, their foundations disturb less ground.

ILLUSTRATIONS

PHOTOGRAPH	PAGE
Coutances Cathedral	4
Stuttgart Airport	5
Bibliothèque Nationale, Paris	11
Willis, Faber & Dumas HQ by day	18
by night	19
Bouhbera, Malta	24
Cloister of the Suleyman Mosque	25
Packwood Gardens	27
Villa Savoye, Poissy	32
Peter Moro's House	33
House at Ojai by Richard Neutra	34
Holy Trinity Church, Dublin	36
Sir Thomas White Building	
St John's College, Oxford	37
Little Moreton Hall, Cheshire	39
17 Queen Anne's Gate, Westminster	40
23 Queen Anne's Gate	41
Bedford Square, London	42
Woburn Walk, London	43
Alton West, Roehampton	47
Granny house, Siphnos	49
House at Apollonia, Siphnos	49
Paddington Station, London	51
S. Geminiano, Tuscany	55
Richards Memorial Centre, Philadelphia	58
Lloyd's of London	61
Seagram Building, New York	62
Los Manantiales, Mexico	64
St Martin's in the Fields	66
Hardwick Hall, Derbyshire	71
Heveningham Hall, Suffolk	75
St Catherine's College, Oxford, dining hall	78
St Catherine's College, Oxford	79
National Theatre, London	82
by night	83
1 Finsbury Avenue, London	86
Surtees' House, Newcastle-upon-Tyne	87
St Göran's Hospital Restaurant, Stockholm	89
Lycée Albert Camus, Fréjus	90
Suleyman Mosque, Istanbul	93
Neue Staatsgalerie, Stuttgart	95
Chiswick House	97
The Economist Building, St James, London	100

DRAWINGS by SIMON WATKINSON

'Shelter can take many forms'	13
Light penetration	15
Design exercise for beginners	17
The human body, basis of all architectural scale	53

ACKNOWLEDGMENTS

I welcome this opportunity to thank all of those friends, institutions, architects, scholars and photographers who have so generously contributed their time, money, patience or encouragement to the production of this book – whose aim is to make the many dimensions of architecture better understood by a wider public.

My thanks to the Building Centre Trust

- to the Architectural Association Foundation for access to the Eric de Maré Archive.
- to Edouard le Maistre, Secretary of the AA; Betty Underwood, Librarian; Valerie Bennett, Slide Librarian; Dennis Crompton and his colleagues in the Print Studio; and all the other members of staff who make the AA a place to raise one's spirits.
- to Andrew Mead, Review and Information Editor of the *Architects' Journal*; Christopher Denver of the Greater London Photograph Library.
- to Kenneth and Adam Rowntree, who helped all the time.
- to: Sasha and Esmond Devas, Monica Pidgeon, Natasha Kroll and Ruth Race, kind hosts in London.
- to John Anstey, Arup Associates, James Austin, Prudence Bliss, Rosemary Burton, Peter Buchan, Lord Bullock, Martin Charles, John Cornforth, David Dunster, Lesley Goodden, Vernon Gracie, Chris Hewison, Anthony Kersting, Deborah Lavin, Sir Denys Lasdun, Deborah Lavin, Robert Maxwell, John Milner, Peter Moro, Carolyn Price, Malcolm Newton, Gordon Ryder, Sir Peter Shepheard, Peter Smithson, Derek Sugden and David West.

THE MUDDLE WE

CHAPTER 1
THE MUDDLE WE FIND OURSELVES IN

People talk about architecture today. The discussion is loud but not clear. This old, rather stiff word has been taken out for an airing and dusted down. This can only be good for it. However, the talking is not the debate it is said to be. No clear proposition is put forward, to be supported or opposed. It is more a matter of taking sides, deciding which team to support.

Are you for Modern or for Post Modern? For new methods or traditional? For 'the community' or for the sinister bureaucrats who want us to live in tower blocks? These vague but very emotive concepts have to do with the trappings and labels of architecture, but they have very little to do with the reality that is its core. Architecture does not need fans. It needs friends who will take the trouble to understand it. It is a complicated art, very rewarding to explore.

This book aims to turn attention away from the styles of Neo this and that, and to show architecture to its well-wishers in its true and wider context, as a means of enhancing life, as a means, perhaps, of enlightenment. The possibilities of architecture always exist within the current social and technological framework, and the limits that this imposes. Many of the people who worry about the state of the art prefer to ignore that framework. While they do this they will be of no help to architecture. There are, of course, many people who are not in the habit of thinking in three dimensions, let alone the six-dimensional world that architects have to operate in.

Admittedly the Battle of the Styles has been a recurring theme of Western architecture. Gothic was upheld in the nineteenth century as the style of spirituality. The eighteenth century adopted Classicism as the true expression of the Enlightenment. We, however, do not live in that century. The period that divides us from it has changed the world more radically than even the pioneers of science could have expected or desired. Mankind has indeed, as bidden, gone forth and multiplied. Our fragile species, bent simply upon survival, has unwittingly transformed itself into the major threat to the survival of the earth itself. Eighteenth-century people travelled on horseback. We can fly faster than sound. In the world of communications Concorde is a Neanderthal.

These two momentous centuries have changed the appearance of buildings, greatly increased their size, and made a nonsense of the way we continue to produce them. It naturally follows that the way they are designed has changed. But has the art of architecture changed

FIND OURSELVES IN

in any essential way? I believe not.

My favourite definition of architecture appeared in a short book written in 1624 by an Englishman, Sir Henry Wotton. He begins as follows:
    'In Architecture as in all the Operative Arts,
        the end must direct the Operation.
            The end is to build well.
        Well building hath three conditions,
          Commoditie, Firmenes and Delight.'

Wotton was translating the words of the Roman architect, Vitruvius – firmitas, utilitas, venustas – written in the first century BC. Today we might say convenience, and stability, but still delight.

What makes people so angry about architecture is the buildings they see. We have every reason to be unhappy to see so many ugly and pretentious buildings spilled with so little architectural expertise over our dwindling supply of virgin land. Take a look around you and the current obsession with past styles, traditional materials that have become impossibly expensive, and past patterns of settlement, is entirely understandable. When you like something it seems reasonable that you will learn by looking at it, that by noticing what old buildings look like you can learn how to build acceptable buildings today. This has manifestly not happened. The reason is that simply to look at those buildings you may happen to pass is too chancy. Buildings have three dimensions in space alone, plus the dimension of time. They need studying, not merely from the outside, but in depth.

I have always thought that most people can recognize a good building when they see it – provided it is not a contemporary building. There are two reasons for this exception. Before the Industrial Revolution and the consequent speeding up of the whole tempo of life, building tradition had proceeded at a very slow pace. Buildings were a simpler proposition than they are today. The second reason has to do with education. Drawing is taught in schools all over the world, but there is no comparable routine to introduce children to the concept of enclosed space. Many people seem to base their architectural expectations on an image like their childish drawings – a cottage with front door in the middle, a window each side and a roof on top. Their archetypal building is cosy and beguiling, nothing like the bank or the garage where they work every day. The snag to a pictorial view of architecture is that, while pictures are in two dimensions, architecture cannot exist in less than three. As children move up the school they learn to convey the third dimension by perspective. One of the things that has happened to buildings is that they have increased in size, and drawing today's large buildings in perspective is a forbidding task. More important, the reason for a building's existence is what happens inside it. Buildings exist to enclose space for use. Architecture is about spaces, and no one bothers to point out to children that space is all around them, that they exist within it. Anyone who has tried to photograph a small room may remember their disappointment with the result, the frustration of seeing such a boring picture of a room that seemed so attractive when one was in it. When you are inside a building it has little resemblance to a drawing. You relate to an enclosed space by moving about in it. You become aware of its existence around and behind you. As you move about a space you seem to become part of it. The fact that your eye cannot be in two places at once brings the dimension of time into architecture. Time is an important factor both in the designing of a building and in the subsequent success or failure of the design. It is only when you realize how many dimensions there are to architecture that the full interest of the subject begins to dawn upon you.

It is paradoxical that architecture has come to be associated with the past, because it can only be designed for use in the future. The fact that the future cannot be fully known, that one is designing for a prediction, must be the cause of some architectural failures, but this cannot be any reason to design for the past, which has no need of buildings. The only certainty about the future is that it cannot repeat the past, since every generation is born into a world that is different. In the past this difference must have been slight, but with the acceleration of life it is increasing, and it is always crucial.

Anyone who is seriously concerned to get better buildings should move into the present because that is the only position in time where designing can be done. Designers have no choice but to work in the present, so anyone wishing to comprehend or influence design must join them there.

Architecture desperately needs the people who talk about it. If we want better buildings, and there is no doubt that formidable numbers of people do, we have first to look at the present situation. Many providers of buildings confuse architecture, which is to them a nebulous idea, with pretension. This is why it often seems that the more you pay for a house the less intelligent thought will have gone into its design.

I suggest that the way to approach the subject of building design is to cool down, to turn not just your eyes but your inquisitive mind to the whole subject of building. I propose some basic questions. Who are buildings for? How are they built? Who builds them? Who pays for them? And, most important of all, what are buildings for?

The answers to these questions may surprise you. They will show you where your interests lie. You may see what action you can take to understand the built world and make it more to your liking. You will certainly be in a better position to ask and consider the question: what is it that makes some buildings architecture?

BIBLIOTHEQUE NATIONALE
PARIS 1854
Architect: Henri Labrouste

Cast iron, a material awaiting the designer to give it form. Its bearing strength and plasticity gave new meaning to the problem of balancing daylight against structure, and offered glimpses of new possibilities – of form, of span, and of ornament. Some exploited them to excess, others began to shape a new architecture.

WHAT ARE

**CHAPTER 2
OUR CONTAINERS**

We build for shelter and security. In high latitudes shelter is mainly a matter of keeping the rain out and the heat in. Traditionally in Britain we think in terms of solid walls and roof. These keep the burglars out while they keep us warm. In the tropics the sun's heat is the enemy. There draughts are not dreaded; they are the breath of life. A continuous current of air has to be coaxed through buildings to temper the humidity and cool the skin – hence the louvres and lacy screens of oriental architecture. The openings have to be small enough to keep out intruders, and their size arrived at by balancing the needs of security against the need for coolness.

This balancing of opposites to provide for conflicting requirements crops up at every stage of building design. First of all the demand for maximum security has to be met within the restrictions of the budget. The demand for ever larger windows clashes with the need for the insulation that solid walls provide. There is the need to keep the weather out while letting the daylight in. Each decision is a balancing act in itself, their sum a very complex equation.

Consider what it is we have to shelter – our lives and all of our activities, work and play, from the nursery to the old people's home. Buildings are the containers of our lives.

Most of our activities need light. Until electric lighting was generally adopted, at the beginning of the twentieth century, the only plentiful light was daylight. It follows that striking the balance between the solid structure needed to support the roof and the voids necessary to let in the daylight was right at the centre of the design process. The resolution of this particular conflict was in fact the hub of architectural design throughout the daylight era.

Shelter can take many forms. The choice of the appropriate form will depend upon the purpose of the building, the local climate, the level of security needed, and the money available. The immense field of choice that conditions building design today is a recent phenomenon. Before the days of steam you built in local materials in the style that had been handed down by the local craftsmen.

In warm climates post-and-beam construction was the convenient way of supporting a roof. This method has produced the measured formality of classical architecture around the Mediterranean sea. Cooler climates are better served by solid walls. And since there is no upper limit to the demand for daylight, windows have grown steadily larger through the centuries as the more adventurous masons and designers tried how far they could pare away the walls.

The drawing overleaf shows how the angle of daylight relates to the width of a building, and how both relate to the ceiling height. Until the

BUILDINGS FOR?

D1. Shelter can take many forms.

massed ranks of mild steel components appeared on the market the majority of roofs were built in timber. This meant that the width of rooms and small buildings was governed by the height of available trees.

So, in addition to the basic planning of spaces and their use, we have already noted four factors that must be taken into account. These are the loads to be carried, the width the timbers can span, daylight, and warmth. None of these factors can be considered on its own; they all interrelate. Nor can any one of them be ignored. For instance, the proportion of void to solid in the external walls depends not only upon the relative importance of daylight and warmth, but also on the load the walls have to carry. The possibility of enlarging the windows by raising the ceiling height depends not only on whether enough money can be found, but also on the level of heat envisaged for those rooms.

You can see that building is a three-dimensional process of some complexity. We all know this, of course, but it is quite usual for people to base their architectural judgements solely on the facades – or even on one facade. Admittedly the outsides of buildings are important to us all, painfully so because they are there and we cannot avoid seeing them. To many dwellers in the duller towns those facades *are* the environment.

Because the facade is so often the only part of a building we see, we tend to forget that it is only a part of something far more interesting. Facades have a two-way relationship with the plans. The pattern made by the arrangement of the windows may be the result of their having been located where light was needed. On the other hand, a pleasing window pattern on elevation may have dictated the plan – not the best way of locating the lighting for someone's home or work place. In three-dimensional thinking, the feedback between the factors of structure, daylighting, planning, and the resulting facades is so rapid and sustained that it feels like a continuous flow, just as a succession of stills is seen as a moving picture.

Three-dimensional thinking does not come naturally to most of us. It cannot simply be memorized, like the basic facts of academic disciplines. A designer learns his skill by designing. Architects learn it over a period of five years, at their drawing boards, on an ascending scale of design, from the design of a kitchen to the planning of a town. This is why their training is so long. The paymasters of education are, naturally, trying to shorten architecture courses, but the pressure is resisted because the profession regards this skill as the essential core of the architect's training.

How then can the layman who loves architecture acquire the habit of mind to juggle with the three – or four or six? – dimensions of this art? I think there has to be a natural aptitude, in amateurs as in architects, a lot of patience and the will to persevere. People who have both the aptitude and a home of their own do get plenty of practice, and learn many lessons about the difficulties of co-ordinating the factors of comfort, convenience, lighting and heating, and combining them into an entity that will be perceived as such. But is this architecture or interior design? It does not matter. The art is the same. Whether you are designing a building or furnishing a room you are designing space for use. The first thing to know is what the space will be used for. Then you have to consider the method of heating and come to terms with the hardware this demands. The only completely invisible heating is underfloor heating. Stoves, radiators and ceiling grilles all have their own uncompromising character, and a limited colour range. Then the acoustic requirements have to be thought out before you choose the surface finishes. Last, and most difficult of all, you have to arrange the daylighting and artificial lighting for every possible contingency. If you succeed in bringing all this together, the character of the place will be

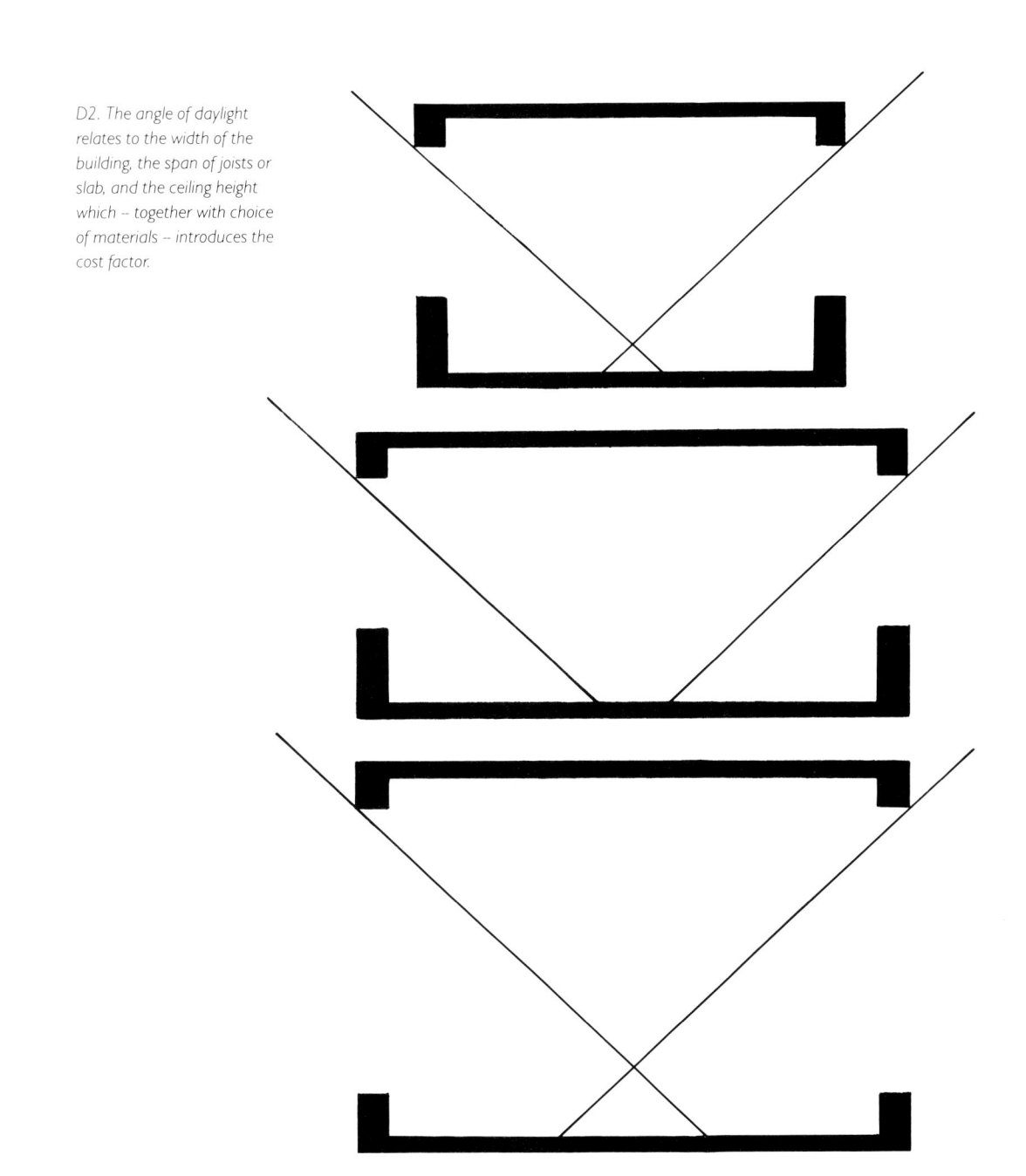

D2. The angle of daylight relates to the width of the building, the span of joists or slab, and the ceiling height which -- together with choice of materials -- introduces the cost factor.

immediately evident, and probably its purpose. If it does not have this coherence, architecturally speaking you will have failed.

If I had to set up a course on the appreciation of architecture, one exercise I would give my students would be to design some small-scale item which nevertheless involved the whole range of design elements: for instance, a set of shelves for the kitchen. This may surprise you if you think that the humbler elements of a place, particularly a 'working' rather than a 'reception' area, do not need designing. But you would be wasting your money if you set out to buy the materials for building your shelves without first having designed them. If you did not know that shelves, like any other three-dimensional artefact, can be constructed in many different ways, and project all sorts of images, you would know better by the time you had made your shopping list. By then you would have had to answer the following questions.

What are the shelves for?
What are they made of?
What length are you considering?
What width will be convenient for what you want to put on them?
What thickness should they be? (This will depend on the distance between supports.)
If the material is to be wood, will it be hardwood, softwood, or chipboard?
If the latter, is it to be painted? If so, what colour?
Will there be much dust around? If so, should you really be designing a cupboard with doors?
Would shelves with glass sliding-doors look more animated?
Will the shelves need ends, or are they to be jointed into vertical boards?
How are they to be supported, with brackets or wall battens?
If brackets, would individual metal brackets or a kit with its own vertical wall fixings be best?

As you answer these questions you will see that none of them makes any sense on its own. The thickness of the shelf depends upon its span, and the placing of the brackets. The questions about materials and finishes are largely aesthetic, and are interdependent. The fixings too, in this instance, are a matter of style. Long before you have considered all the answers you will see that the questions fall into two groups. Some are purely practical, others involve subtleties of expression. That is where the architecture comes in. You select the bracket and fixing that most clearly marks the purpose and meaning of the building, and the designer's attitude to it. In this way you build up the integrity of a design.

The sculptor feels out the contours of his work with sharp blows of the hammer and chisel. The painter creates an impression of light with innumerable brush strokes. The architect animates the inert materials of his building by giving his full attention first to the selection, and then to the joining, of every component. Where glass meets its frame, where the plaster arrives at the door jamb, how far the shelf should oversail the bracket, is the stuff of this art. Tradition is there as a yardstick. It exists, not to be copied, but as a signpost and a challenge. What next? What is appropriate *today*? The task is to keep the weather out, but the question of exactly how to do this can produce some marvellous answers.

Buildings can be thought of as protective shells or as envelopes enclosing the structure. The idea of the shell seems to fit in with the increasing role security plays in our calculations. There was a time when security, for domestic buildings, was thought of mainly in terms of theft, but today the idea of being attacked in one's home can no longer be dismissed as fantasy. There is a case for the shell as a metaphor, but I prefer the envelope. Most architects do, because they are anxious to display the spaces that are the meaning of the building. A building

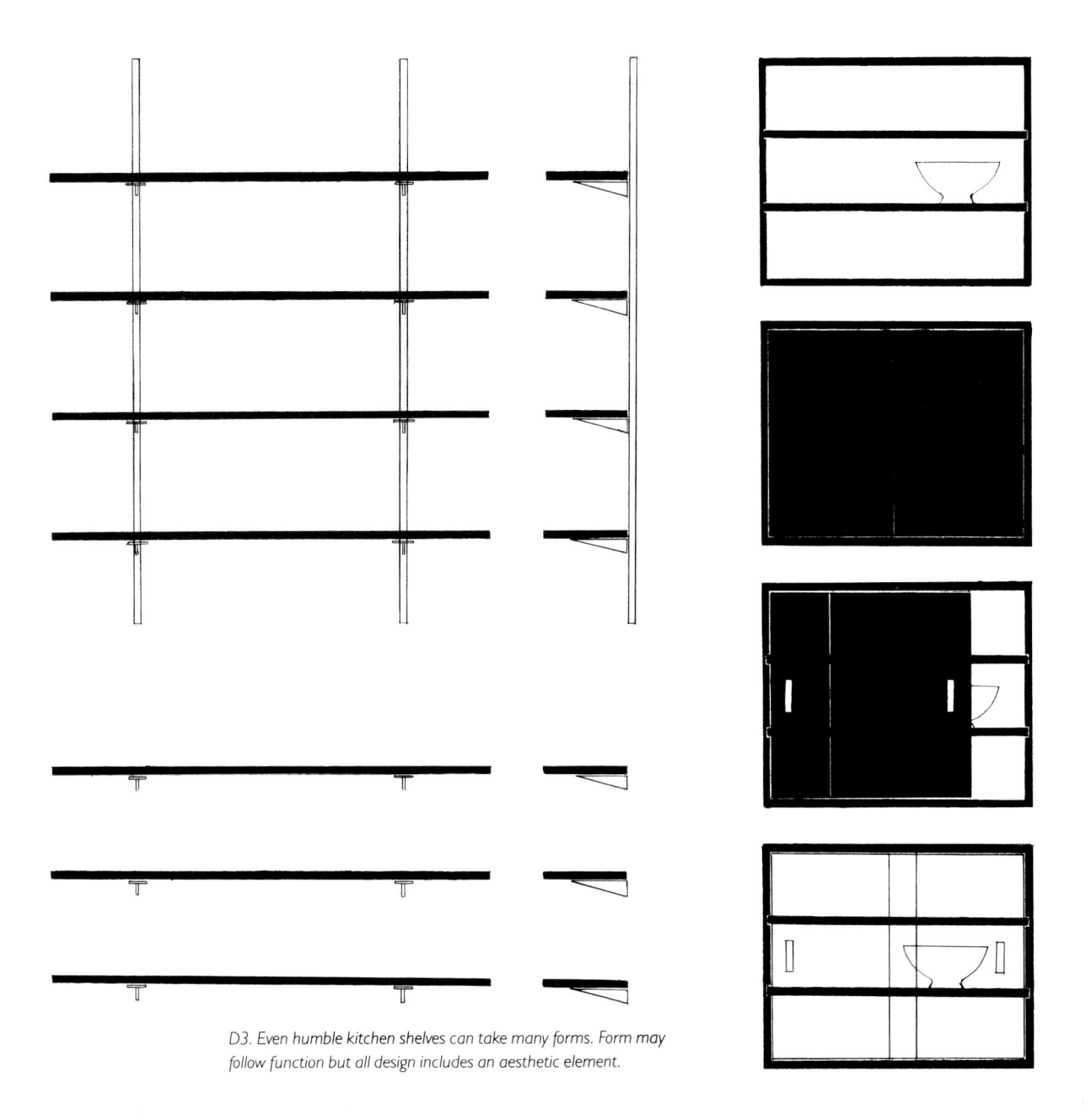

D3. Even humble kitchen shelves can take many forms. Form may follow function but all design includes an aesthetic element.

Head Office for
WILLIS, FABER & DUMAS
IPSWICH, SUFFOLK 1975
Architects and engineers:
Foster Associates

This building, 'consisting of skin and bone', fulfils a prophecy by Mies van der Rohe. And by night it reveals lighted interiors.

WILLIS, FABER & DUMAS
by day

The building stands on the edge of the old town, offering a shifting panorama of its neighbourhood.

may have to repel intruders, but it can still display its uses and its character. Until the Willis Faber building appeared in Ipswich the architecture of financial buildings had always been a moneyed deadpan. By replacing the traditional masonry with a suspended glass facade that reflected or revealed according to the strength of the daylight, Norman Foster showed that to invite inspection could be a way of displaying confidence.

Nevertheless, neither metaphor fits the case. Both are misleading because they are only skin deep, whereas my whole purpose is to emphasize the three-dimensional nature of buildings. The solid form of a building would perhaps be more appropriately represented by an egg box, shaped to protect its fragile contents while offering surfaces for display.

I mentioned that the fourth dimension is time. Time is involved in any use of a building, and spaces can only be experienced by moving through them and about them. Any movement is a movement in time. And then there is always the construction time. There is bound to be a sizeable lapse of time between the commissioning of a building and the final handover because the building has to be designed and built, let alone financed.

The designer has to work in the present, but the building he is planning and specifying will only exist in the future, and the future cannot be fully known.

A great deal *is* known about a building. The owner certainly knows, often very precisely, why he is embarking upon such a demanding task. The architect will, as part of his job, research the processes the building is to house. He will compile the contract documents, whose aim is precision. Nevertheless, the most important factor in the success of any building is the skill of its promoters and designer in anticipating what the future will need.

There is a fifth vital dimension to buildings, which, as everybody knows, is cost. The quality of architecture has an important relationship with cost, but that is not to say that the higher the cost of the building the better it will be as architecture. A work of architecture need not be expensive; what it needs is to be conceived in relation to the money available. The most striking example that comes to my mind is a two-roomed house designed for Mexican peasant families. The architects had dispensed with the luxury of doors, the roof was corrugated iron and the kitchen was a veranda. But this house had what it needed to make a graceful and inviting home in that climate – more than many a house whose mortgage is going to turn its owners into slaves. The clarity and concern that had gone into the planning and detailing of this minimal dwelling had made it a work of architecture.

When we design these containers to live and work in, the menace is that they can mould our lives and constrict our activities. They can, on the other hand, enhance the life that goes on in them, and it is the potential to do this that makes the long and tedious routines of architectural practice worthwhile.

Architects have tradition to guide them and the abundance of industrial production to draw upon, but in using this know-how and these commodities, an architect has to take a step, however small, towards the future. The word 'tradition' is slung about today with the accent all on the past, yet the word means 'handing on' and that requires judgement and commitment. When we embark upon a journey there is always the possibility of disaster, yet we all set out expecting to arrive. It is the same when you are geared to the future. The risk of failure is implicit, and we know that some buildings do fail, both to keep the rain out and to give satisfaction as a place to inhabit or enjoy. However, it is still imperative that architects look to the future rather than the past, because the future is where their buildings are going to be.

CHAPTER 3
THE BUSINESS OF BUILDING

Building is a business. Its bulky products are assembled by human skills. These skills emerge from two different traditions: the crafts that are almost as old as history, and the technologies that date from the first attempts to harness natural forces to provide water, light and power.

We speak of the 'building industry', but owing to the intimate relationship buildings have with the ground they stand on, the complete package of building processes has never been fully industrialized. The building elements most firmly anchored in the earth are foundations and drainage. Even mobile homes prefer their drains and services to be dug in. The range of piped, wired and ducted services becomes more sophisticated every year. The addition of electronics to a normal building's equipment sharpens the contrast with functions like excavating and pile driving. Half a century ago an ex-midshipman who was working on a building site became so obsessed by the contrast between the happy-go-lucky manner in which America approached housing design and the high precision of its weapons programme that he became the lifelong, itinerant prophet of industrialized building. Buckminster Fuller's vision of a building industry organized to meet the world's housing needs has not – even half a century later – been realized. The best that can be said is that some of the richer nations have managed to organize their building operations to function efficiently.

In America more co-operation exists, and less confrontation, between the design and construction teams. In Britain things can go very well when the best firms are working on prestigious buildings. Those wishing to embark on minor works must take what they can get. Not only the components of the buildings but the men who build them are of two kinds and from two cultures. The industrial components emerge identical and, at least in theory, quality controlled. On delivery, these products face the daily hazards of the building site, where a dim man in the wrong place can defeat precision planning at any hour of the day. Meanwhile, the presence on site of joiners, brick-layers and labourers offers a facility for adaptation which, although in theory archaic, is constantly in demand.

The joiner who fixes the factory-made windows has the skills to make those windows himself – but not so cheaply. He is the direct cultural descendant of the carpenters on whom building construction depended before the Fire of London underlined the necessity for using less combustible materials. The same goes for the plasterer engaged in pinning up plasterboard for skimming. Not so for the electrician. Whereas the efficiency of oil lamps had been developed over centuries, electric lighting is still immature. Its technology has developed from the first electric light to the wiring of a submarine in little more than a century. Demand has far outstripped both theory and design. The electrician and the heating engineer belong to a modern workforce of short tradition and high specialization. They are numerate and geared to the future. They feel a responsibility to the firm of subcontractors that employs them rather than to the building on which they happen to be working.

This dichotomy stems from the fact that the building crafts and trades have not yet succeeded in coalescing into a single entity. When this happens the industry will be better tuned to the needs of the buildings themselves and the intentions of their design. While the wired and electronic services become more adaptable every year, the muddy realities of site work – and the constant need for building repairs – keep the antique community of small builders muddling along as their forefathers did.

Wherever the craft and precision cultures coexist, the dichotomy complicates the training of architects and makes architecture a complex career. It also confuses clients and the way they judge architects and their work. The public blames architects for what it sees as a falling away from the good old craft traditions. It also blames the use of new materials for the shortage of good architecture. This is a fundamental misunderstanding. Many people think that the stone facing that covers the lightweight insulation blocks on the 'luxury homes' is architecture. Fine architecture depends on nothing but the architect's ability and integrity. It can be made of concrete or of stone, of mud or corrugated iron. The idea that architecture can be slipped onto a building like an overcoat is simple ignorance. Architecture is either present from the designer's first doodle to the final production drawings or it is not there at all. It is always the realization of a comprehensive idea. By the same token, this paragraph may seem to be a digression into architecture from a chapter on building, but it hardly can be because you cannot separate the two.

With components as likely to come from Taiwan as from Birmingham, documentation has become essential. To assemble the necessary hardware in the right sequence for its construction into a building – let alone the particular building that is described in the contract documents – is an astonishing feat of management. These components can come from anywhere in the world. They have to be transported to the site and, once there, protected – from theft, carelessness, changes in temperature or humidity, and other accidents. The contractor has to programme for deliveries to be met by appropriate fitters from his own or from his subcontractors' workforce, and this programme needs continuous adjustment as dates slip and targets are not met. And this is not to mention changes to the design by client, architect or subcontractor. For these reasons the kind of manager needed in building needs all the education he can possibly get, from an apprenticeship to a Master's degree in Management. In Britain such managers are still a little thin on the ground. No doubt this is due in part to the discomforts of the building site in such a climate, which many intelligent young people prefer to avoid. I believe it is also partly due to the emphasis on literary as against visual skills in the educational tradition, and partly to the low status the culture accords to manual work. I have noticed, too, that the type of mind that finds it natural to think in three dimensions – the type that is a godsend on a building site – is not the type that makes a high grade manager. It just does not occur to school leavers with management potential to apprentice themselves to a trade. This tends to make the system self perpetuating. It means that managers have to be brought in to building from other fields, and will therefore have to catch up on site experience. They are also likely to feel more at home with the technological members of the workforce than with the traditional tradesmen. In fact the major task awaiting the new managers is to replace the ancient loyalties of the different trades and the new technologies by focusing the attention of the entire workforce on the building under construction and its purposes.

Building construction is a high risk business. The profit margin, and hence a firm's survival, is constantly critical. No doubt a firm's reputation rests ultimately upon the standards it offers, so that maintenance of standards is vital to its long-term interests. Today, unfortunately, we live in a short-sighted era. Cash flow and immediate financial viability take precedence. It is not the fault of building contractors that this has become a fact of life. It is a most unwelcome fact to builders, as it is to architects. Contractors are constantly under pressure to put cash flow before workmanship. This shifts their share of responsibility on to the shoulders of the architect, thereby undermining the intention of the contract, which was drafted to ensure that the contractor was responsible for his work. It is also abrasive to architecture, which depends upon precise detailing and, to some extent, upon 'well building'. In a situation where a contractor feels bound to put speed before workmanship, very little time will be spent checking the work against the drawings. It will be left to the architect to refuse completed work, a much more costly matter for the contractor, and hence a duty the architect would rather avoid. It places architect and builder, who need to work together, on different sides.

Both contractors and building owners depend upon the arcane world of building finance. This includes banks, building societies, insurance companies, government departments, property developers and charities such as preservation trusts. Some follow these callings as a business, some as a profession, some as a vocation – and some as a crime. Building owners have to borrow very large sums; contractors borrow, of course, on a regular basis. Public authorities assume different roles at different times, sometimes making grants on a statutory, sometimes on a discretionary, basis.

Buildings are ferocious consumers of money, or you can say with equal truth that building is a major field of investment. These two statements represent a tension that is a permanent feature of building finance. The banking institutions seem to take the fact that time is money to mean that the design and construction of buildings should proceed at headlong speed. They ignore the equally important fact that time spent on design and on conforming with good building practice is money soundly invested. It is hard to avoid the inference that, where building is concerned, banks, building societies and insurance companies see themselves in a business rather than a professional role. They appear to be concerned with short-term gain rather than with wise investment.

The myopic vision of building financiers leads to a questionable investment policy, because it hustles builders and tempts them to cut corners. Moreover, it is inimical to architecture because it threatens the quality not only of the building fabric but of the design as well. As the designer's ideas emerge, time is needed to bring the spatial, structural and social demands of the project into balance, to let the dust of creative excitement settle, and to explore the implications of the theme. In the case of large buildings the design team will also be large and may consist of more than one professional firm. Communication takes time. This is a field in which best results cannot be hurried. Nevertheless, architects are constantly urged to hurry, to set optimistic programmes and to speed up the production information. Yet this information is the building owner's guarantee that he will get the building he is paying for.

All of these applied pressures act upon integrity – the integrity not only of architect and contractor but of the building itself. When an architect is disgraced, or a builder bankrupt, or when a building collapses, there is a public outcry – usually directed at the architects. There are indeed greedy architects, and dishonest builders, but it is my belief that many of these tragedies are the result of failure to resist pressures to build too cheaply and too fast. Does this pressure originate with the lender or the borrower? Is it explicitly stated or merely implicit in the attitude of those who negotiate loans? It may even be a matter of the entire culture which conditions us to judge firms and enterprises by the figures in the annual accounts. If so, is this a sensible way to evaluate a building? The value of a building lies in what it offers to users, its effect upon the wider community, and how well it succeeds in keeping the rain out for as long as it may stand. I do not think that the designed life of a building is ever less than sixty years, and you have only to look around the older cities to see that it can extend for centuries. What balance sheet can serve as a guide to these three factors?

I have stressed the pressure on the building trades and on the profession of architecture.

What about the art of architecture? How does our present ethos of the fast buck affect this art?

A FORTIFIED MANOR HOUSE, BOUHBERA, MALTA
Seventeenth century

This corner turret, one of four, was presumably a lookout post, possibly defensive cover. Evidently designed by a mason who delighted in his skill, it is a joy to behold.

Cloister of the
SULEYMAN MOSQUE
ISTANBUL 1550
Architect: Koka Sinan

The brick ornament is finely balanced between ingenuity and simplicity, but the impact, both of the cloister and of the great building of which it is part, is of an unquestionable rightness.

CHAPTER 4
THE ART OF ARCHITECTURE

Architecture is the art of enclosing space. The word suggests distance and breadth, even freedom, but what makes space so uniquely valuable to us human beings is surely that it is the medium we inhabit. Designing buildings – and house hunting – bring home to us how valuable it is. The smaller the space one is concerned with, the more expertly it needs to be planned. Looking at old buildings one can see that cramped conditions have always been the norm. It is this, perhaps, that gives wide open spaces and distant planets their magnetic appeal.

Architecture is, like most arts, an art of organization. The architect's first, and by far his most important concern, is to organize the sequence of spaces to be enclosed – their dimensions, and their function and form in relation to each other. Space is usually defined by walls, roof and floor, but it can be done by hedges, grass and trees. Whether the sequence of spaces is indoors or out, the art is the same – to realize a three-dimensional concept in solid form.

Think for a moment of space as a concept, how sinuous and nebulous it seems, the direct opposite of a walled enclosure. One begins to understand the theory that space is curved, because curves, particularly irregular curves, seem less inimical to the free-flowing character of space than flat planes. The advantage of flatness only becomes evident at the stage when furniture has to be chosen and accommodated. The fact is that some activities need rectilinear enclosures, while others are enhanced by an irregular setting. Swimming is an example. Swimmers in training need parallel lanes, while children and leisurely pursuits can gain from the unexpected.

However the spaces are defined, their forms and relationships are at the heart of architecture. Do you line up your rooms in a row, or let them radiate from a centre? Do you express their relationships and relative importance by different levels and angles? Other factors immediately present themselves. A building in the form of a cube loses heat more slowly than a long narrow one, but if you are relying on daylight the narrow one will be lighter. The sequence of spaces is the weightiest of the whole complex of ingredients that has to be considered, and brought into balance, in any serious attempt at building design.

We can throw some light upon the nature of the architect's art by contrasting it with the sculptor's. The sculptor is creating an object that will exist in space. For the architect the space *is* the object. He is enclosing space to shelter some activity from the weather. It may be a family's life, or an assembly line, or something far more complex, a university perhaps, or a zoo. Some buildings are mainly concerned with the mind and spirit: consider a cathedral – a greenhouse for souls.

Architecture originates in the mind but it exists in buildings, in spaces and in the structure that defines them.

It begins with the jostle and flow of ideas – ideas about the flow of space and the building's purposes; about the flow of water and heat, of pipes and wires; and the converse flow of sewage and dust and garbage being carried away. Always central to this flow of ideas is the building's future activity, the flow and jostle of the people for whom it is being designed.

When a novel is printed the flow of ideas that the author finally selected can be followed across its pages. Not so with a building. I suppose one might follow the correspondence through the files, and later through the drawings and specification. But finally, after the battles and compromises, the balancing and trimming and adjustment, the architect can only make his point in the silence of geometry, in the meeting of planes and the contrast of textures. The observer of buildings is offered no linear thread to guide him.

The link between the darting and wheeling of

THE GARDENS OF PACKWOOD HOUSE, WARWICKSHIRE 1660

'Space is usually enclosed by walls, roof and floor, but it can be done by hedges, grass and trees.'
John Fetherston, owner of Packwood, stayed at home and laid out his gardens during the dangerous years of the Commonwealth.

the stream of consciousness and the rigid fabric of the ensuing building is order. The flow of the activities to be housed determines the natural sequence of the building's spaces, but they can only be built in this simple, two-dimensional sequence if the site is extensive enough. Otherwise the architect will have to adapt the linear pattern to the three-dimensional possibilities. The task is to enclose the spaces and support a roof, but it is in the way he chooses to engineer this transformation that the architect can realize the spirit of the project and give substance to its promoters' intentions and hopes. This is where talent is needed. Though the uncompromising components of building can hardly be more unlike the insubstantial stuff ideas are made of, some minds can make them the rich, strange fabric of architecture.

All buildings are not architecture. Some aspire to be, some intend to be but have the wrong idea. I am writing, as others have done, to explore what this mysterious ingredient is. It certainly has to do with the design rather than the soundness of the building work, or even the beauty of the materials. All over Britain today you can see examples of expensive housing – 'Executive Housing' is its label – where good quality materials have been insisted on. The planners have demanded this with the best of motives, to produce beauty, even specifically to produce architecture. In many cases these costly materials have been used to construct dwellings that are more ugly, more grotesque in their misunderstanding of traditional architecture than anything ever built before. This ugliness and vulgarity does not come from shoddy workmanship or cheap materials, so it is clearly to do with the design and layout of the buildings.

One can dislike a building while conceding that it is architecture. Architecture does not consist in prettiness and belongs to no one style. It is a result of the designer's skill – not his ability to get the building finished on time and within the contract sum, important though this is, but his ability to plan in as many dimensions as are needed, and to produce a single entity out of a mountain of hardware. And there is something harder to define, a palpable quality of enhancement. Henry Wotton called it delight, Norman Foster calls it joy.

The Gothic cathedrals are striking examples of this quality, as they are of everything that is important in architecture. Their impact is total and immediate. You have only to enter and the whole building acts upon you, body and mind. You draw breath. You look up. There is excitement in the way the light falls, and at the same time a holy quiet. The building was no doubt planned like any other to accommodate a congregation of a known size; the monastic and lay communities balanced in chancel and nave, the columns regularly spaced to take the load. As this building form took root and developed, the third dimension, height, was exploited ever more daringly, to lift the consciousness of the congregation above the day's concerns, and free their spirits to soar. Decorated these buildings certainly are, some more than others, but I do not think anyone would dispute that space is what their architecture is about.

Although I believe that the art of architecture today is the same as it was in Gothic times, the procedures now used to produce it are very different. In those days the architect was working with local craftsmen in local materials, with a long tradition to guide him. He had to combine the skills of masons, carpenters, glaziers, roofers and plasterers, some of whom he could rely on for creative detailing that was to become a part of the building's glory. I have already outlined the situation we have today, in which the traditional building trades and the technological work force have not arrived at a common culture. Naturally this dichotomy affects architectural practice. The architect can select many of a building's components from the immense resources of industry, but since he is aiming at a seamless character for his building rather than an approximation, many components still have to be designed in his office. Although selection from the international market is a formidable task, it is still secondary to the architect's creative function. The design must be so firmly based on the intention and purposes of the building that it can guide a team of architects and engineers, not only through the design stage, but through all the problems that may arise during the contract period. Some of these are quite unforeseeable as they can result from commercial and political developments that occurred after the contract was signed.

Buildings today vary so greatly in size that it is impossible to describe architectural practice in a way that applies equally to a cottage and an office block. When I speak of the design team I intend no disparagement of the one-man practice, or laymen who design their own buildings. Architecture does not have to be produced by architects, although I think it is true to say that the proportion of buildings that turn out to be architecture is higher among those designed by architects than among those that were not. There are incompetent architects just as there are incompetent dentists and solicitors. And there are engineers, journalists and housewives whose designs have the sure touch of art. To make architecture you do not have to have a degree or diploma. What you do have to have is a compelling interest in buildings and how they are put together, and the energy to worry out the details and hunt for components that are perfectly in character.

The American architect, Louis Kahn, used to urge students to 'try to find out what the building wants to be'. I would acknowledge Kahn's stature on the strength of that remark alone. It puts an attitude that is essential to the making of architecture into words that anyone can understand. This is a commitment to a building as something that exists in its own right, like a child. It is not going to belong wholly to its owner, certainly not to its architect, but will be there to be lived in and looked at in the unpredictable future.

The art of enclosing space can only be pursued through the business and the technologies of building, and with the co-operation of building financiers. It is hard to express how cumbersome an art it is. Even the design stage involves more than one profession – architects, surveyors, engineers of several kinds, and landscape architects. When it comes to the production drawings there are innumerable manufacturers to deal with, and later, on site, an army of tradesmen and technicians, not to mention labourers. These are admittedly the contractors' responsibility. Nevertheless, they are all engaged in making or marring the one design. This is an art by remote control. The architect's tools may initially be pencils, models and computers, but the work of art he is engaged in will be constructed, from start to finish, by other people, many of whom he will never meet. He has to ensure that it will be buildable – by others; that it will be affordable – by others.

The process by which an architect sets about ensuring that groups of strangers will indeed produce the work of art he has designed is long and tedious. The entire building, in all its detail, has to be drawn. The only way to make your building sing out loud and clear is to make sure that every detail is described – the pattern of the paving on the terrace, the louvres in the window of the shower. Every item has to be specified in such a way that all the possible variants, except the one selected, are excluded. To people who think of art in terms of paint or clay all this may not sound particularly artistic. Nevertheless, all art does depend upon precision. Manual and chromatic precision is the watercolourist's skill. Architectural precision is, not surprisingly, quite different in kind. It is more akin to the precision of the translator, a precision that is the result of a multi-faceted awareness of intention, of nuances and of rhythm.

Drawings, however detailed, and models, however accurate, are still very small in scale compared with the buildings they represent. Until a building is built no one can experience its spaces, because they are nowhere defined in space. At the design stage the building exists only as an idea. This idea must be so real to the design team that they can match samples and colours to it, even though it includes wholly imaginary elements. The most important of these is the vision of its future occupants at work or play. The designer visiting showrooms or searching through catalogues does not so much select as recognize the right component, which is the one that assimilates instantly into the idea of the building. This applies just as much to the team of architects working on a large scheme as to an individual designing a house. An architect building up a team selects its members because they see architecture as he does – or at least that is his aim. In practice, few teams remain exactly of one mind. Bright people move on to further their careers and have to be replaced rapidly. A lazy architect lacking this necessary commitment can cause nasty flaws in a building. Aesthetic differences cause less trouble than a lack of commitment or stamina because they rise to the surface and can be argued and agreed. The direction of any architectural design needs to be tested in argument.

Not only are buildings constructed by remote control, at drawing board stage they are also remote in time. Before a building can exist in solid form it has to be designed, receive planning approval, be put out to tender and built. This lapse of time, something between six months and four years, not only affects the components, which may be dearer and harder to get in three years' time than when they were specified. It also affects the reception of the building – by the owner, the building's users and the public at large. Fashion is bound to alter, and the swirl of fashion is rather like the weather; all the evidence may suggest that the depression will deepen, but instead it fills. International developments can also be shattering. Buildings completed in 1974, when oil prices rocketed, had heating systems that were already out of date at handover. There is no way to avoid risks of this kind because the future is a constant factor in building. Time is architecture's fourth dimension. Even if it did not take time to produce a building, the whole of any building's working life must still be in the future.

The fifth dimension is cost. I have already shown how the attitudes of the financial world exert pressures that are inimical both to good workmanship and to design. There are other aspects of the cost factor that the architecture-loving public cannot afford to ignore.

Building is such a costly activity that not everyone can afford even to consider engaging in it. In the highly industrialized countries any building carried out by people in the lower income brackets will have to be self-built. Plenty of Australians and Americans are ready to build their own homes. Not so in Britain, where most buildings are funded commercially. Nations with a large body of historic buildings now find it necessary to support the repair and rehabilitation of these buildings from public funds. This means that much of the built fabric in such countries is more accountable to the public than is generally realized. As shareholders or taxpayers we may have contributed to the very building that we deplore. Activists who kick up a fuss about architectural monstrosities may in fact be minding their own business. They may themselves have a stake in the obnoxious pile. Or they may object to the nation wasting money on something they think it cannot afford. Perhaps such activists could intervene more effectively, and unobtrusively, at an earlier stage? Their pension funds or private holdings may have paid for the developments springing up around them. Or government money, in the form of conservation or development grants, may have passed through their hands.

It is always easier to complain about architecture than to wield such powers as we possess, including our democratic rights. Local authorities in Britain have distributed millions of pounds in grants over the last fifty years, yet architecture is very poorly represented in the Council Chambers. Nor is this important art well served there at the humbler levels of lobbying and bringing pressure to bear, as it is in America. Admittedly the tasks of democracy are, like the practice of architecture, long and tedious. Voting by portfolio, that is to say attending the AGM of companies in which you have an interest, is less time consuming. The snag is that the tendency of industry to arrange itself in ever larger groups makes it extremely difficult to know precisely what one is investing in. It is laborious to tease out the full extent of financial ramifications, but it is perfectly possible. It is obvious that those people who are truly interested in architecture should put their money where their mouths are. Obvious, too, that we should all shoulder those democratic privileges that we hear so much about, by sitting on committees and wielding what clout we can.

Since buildings contain people, architecture clearly has a social dimension. The walls that shelter and enclose us inevitably shape and often constrict our lives. Social change is a major cause of change in the form of buildings, and architects' sensitivity to social change is one of the factors that edges architecture forward. The dramatic change that occurred when the supply of domestic servants was diverted into factories during the First World War is a very potent example. Architects were confronted with the challenge of reinventing the family house. The flexibility that reinforced concrete offered allowed them to meet this challenge in ways that would earlier have been unimaginable, and the process has continued from the time of Frank Lloyd Wright up until the appearance of Arthur Quarmby's underground dwellings. The sheer range of possibility in this familiar territory is still astonishing us.

Architecture's three spatial dimensions are concerned with size. The more interesting, subtle and elusive aspect of size is scale, which is a matter of the relationship between sizes. The scale of a building is established by the relationship of the parts to the whole, and of its apparent size as seen in its surroundings. It is not only the structural units, the bricks and lintels, that establish scale. The door and window openings, the panels and tiles that form its skin, the spacing of balusters and the projection of eaves all play their part. So does a building's relationship with the landscape it stands in, or with the street or group of buildings of which it *appears* to be a part. For even if a building has no functional relationship with its neighbours, it will still establish a relationship in the eye of the beholder. In this relationship scale is all important, because it depends not upon the designer's intention, but upon the viewer's response.

It strikes me that the late twentieth century passer-by does take a very narrow view of what constitutes art. So many seem weighed down by their expectations and preconceptions. So few appear to have been educated to look at a view or a group of buildings to see *what they have to say for themselves*. In order to relate to its neighbours a building does not have to copy their materials or outdated methods. A glass facade can relate very precisely to a medieval stone building – by its scale alone, by proportions, by line, by every device, in fact, of visual art. Contrast can be as telling as resemblance. People accept dramatic contrasts in old buildings – the view of Lincoln cathedral, for instance, across a haphazard foreground of forgotten roofs. It is when the contrast introduces

VILLA SAVOYE, POISSY, FRANCE 1926
Architect: Le Corbusier

This design was the result of Le Corbusier's ten-year struggle to formulate 'la maison de l'époque machiniste'. The motor car presented domestic architects with a central problem. Its size, its swirling path and dangerous speed were a challenge to the scale and existing form of houses. Le Corbusier's response was to enclose the entire volume of the living space in a broad shallow box and raise it on slender 'pilotis' above the dust and hazards of the driveway. The simple packaging served a second purpose, by setting the various elements of family living free to assume the forms appropriate to their different functions.

ARCHITECT PETER MORO'S HOUSE, BLACKHEATH, LONDON 1957

Peter Moro adopted Le Corbusier's strategy for this smaller town house, raising the family's flat above the territory of guests, laundry and motor car.

Whenever space was at a premium, architects of the Modern Movement planned the living areas as a flowing sequence in order to make the most of space, daylight and views. This house received light from all sides – east for the bedrooms, south for the living area, west for dining and north for the kitchen, which opened off the dining area. Only bedrooms and bathrooms were enclosed.

HOUSE AT OJAI, CALIFORNIA 1950s
Architect: Richard Neutra

The development of window glass in the twentieth century offered the interiors of buildings a new relationship with outdoor space and with the distant landscape.

something new that they tend to panic. It is true that architecture can hit you between the eyes. This is why, in Britain, where the culture leans heavily on the past, it is the most imaginative and creative architecture that gets the rudest reception. Quite the opposite in America, where novelty is all. Yet, although these reactions are so different, I believe they stem from the same causes. I think the mulish attitude of the British, and the American pursuit of the new, both result from a discrepancy amounting to contrast between the tempo of the human mind and that of the electronic age we are living in. The technologies that have replaced the architect's bonds with traditional building, and confronted him instead with multiple choice, have done the same for his public. Some refuse the challenge of the new and continue to judge the buildings they see by inappropriate standards, while those stouter spirits who advocate the new will accept everything in sight.

Any new artefact as complicated as a building deserves, at the very least, a long, cool look before assessment. To appreciate architecture you need your sanity. You need also to be aware of the spatial and social dimensions of the art you are assessing. We have not yet touched on the relation of light to architecture, nor the questions of who buildings are for, who pays for them and whose responsibility they are. None of these questions is simple.

We spend so much of our lives in buildings that it is surely of the first importance to consider what effect these buildings are likely to have upon us, for better or for worse. This is why thought should be lavished on their design, far beyond the calculation of short-term profits. This means that unless an owner is prepared to invest his own time and effort in the design, an architect is needed for all stages of both design and construction.

The people inside a building need a place to delight them as well as one that has been designed for its purpose. The recurring delight will enhance their lives. The thoughtful design will make it easier to run and to clean. In the case of a workplace it is likely to increase output, and so make all the difference between profit and loss, between success and failure. The people outside need buildings that will make the environment delightful, too. When you build, whether you intend it or not, you are building for more than your profits, your family or your comfort. You are building for a time-span you cannot know. My house or your factory may stand on its site, raising someone's spirits, or lowering them, for generations – perhaps for centuries – to come.

HOLY TRINITY CHURCH, GRANGEMOUTH, DUBLIN 1980
Architects: A. and D. Wejchert

While winning an Archdiocesian competition for a cut-price church, the Wejcherts managed to achieve a prodigious sense of scale, both from a distance and at the centre of the interior, which none the less retained a feeling of intimacy. The building is said to give a sense of immediacy to the liturgy.

SIR THOMAS WHITE BUILDING for
ST JOHN'S COLLEGE OXFORD 1976
Architect and engineers: Arup Associates

The full height and width of the study bedroom – rather than a small window pane – set the scale for this residential block. The largeness of scale is achieved by emphasizing the building's reinforced-concrete frame. Oxford tradition favours staircases rather than corridors. Here the staircases rise from a covered way whose casual mood – engineered by splays and angles – tempers the rigidity of the cellular facade.

CHAPTER 5
THE PLAY OF MASSES BROUGHT TOGETHER IN LIGHT

Light is the breath of architecture. It is vital to this art in so many ways that it demands a chapter to itself.

A remark of Louis Kahn's was an eye-opener to me. 'Le Corbusier,' he said, 'is very conscious of light. Le Corbusier is thoroughly an architect.' Kahn was quite right; you could not be thoroughly an architect without that consciousness. And sure enough, it is a phrase of Corb's in praise of some building's geometry that I want to quote: 'the masterly, correct and magnificent play of masses *brought together in light*'. It is true that, since architecture is appreciated mainly by eye, you do need light to see it by, but light is a part of the design long before there is any building to see. As soon as an architect gets an idea how to roof a space he has to face the question 'where is the daylight to come from?' This tension between the demands of structure and of daylighting surfaced on the very first page of my chapter exploring the nature of buildings, and questions of lighting will never be far below the surface of the argument.

Not only does light have a dual role – being crucial in arriving at the appropriate form, and also in enabling that form and the spaces it defines to be seen – it is also needed in two kinds, natural and artificial.

Until this century no form of artificial lighting came anywhere near the strength of daylight, even poor daylight. Now the technology can offer any level of light that is needed by industry, commerce, or even surgery and optical research. Artificial light has also the advantage of being perfectly static – but this is also its drawback. The changing angle and unpredictable variety of daylight is, for us human beings, a life-enhancing necessity.

The ability to adjust to whatever light is available has enabled our species to survive so far, but at the present stage of evolution it has become a handicap. For the eye not only has this ability, it also likes to exercise it. Moreover, the eye is linked to another highly evolved mechanism, the brain. Although the bright light of the fluorescent firmament has done wonders for productivity, we are becoming increasingly aware that eye and brain meter the time they care to spend under such *un*demanding conditions. What revenge may these delicate censors exact for eight hours of the tedium of unwavering brightness?

When the possibilities of electric lighting first began to dawn upon mankind they must have seemed an unmixed blessing; but not I think to architects. Their involvement with lighting will have alerted them to the fact that round-the-clock working would uncouple our way of life from the rhythms of the planet to which evolution had designed us. Modern buildings can provide us with comfortable warmth, and light us through the hours of darkness, but in compensating for the inadequacies of daylight they deprive us of a stimulus and a respite that we are programmed to need.

Even by modern standards the human eye has an astonishing ability to adjust. Sunlit snow is a billion times brighter than starlit sky, yet our eyes can adapt so as to be able to see at both of these levels. We may prefer a 500 watt bulb for fine work, but we can if necessary do the work by the light of a few candles. This ability to adapt is just one of the factors that make it more difficult to design the artificial lighting for a building than the daylighting.

Most interiors have a number of uses, and the lighting design must provide for them all. The eye, however, can only adapt to one level at a time, so the lighting for the different uses of an interior must be fairly near in level. The trouble is that the nearer you get to a constant level, the more likely that it will seem monotonous.

There is another problem arising from the eye's adaptability. In artificial lighting schemes the sources of light have to be accommodated within the space to be lit. If you look directly at a

LITTLE MORETON HALL, CHESHIRE

This sixteenth-century house looks as though it has been assembled entirely from very small pieces. Smallest of all are the leaded panes, cunningly cut to form patterned rectangles, which are then assembled into windows of a useful size.

light source your pupil contracts so that you cannot see anything less bright. The sources of light have therefore to be kept out of everyone's line of sight, and the smaller the space the more difficult this becomes. It is easier to meet the functional demands of the large spaces in commercial or industrial buildings than the many conflicting demands of the small family living room. The lower the ceiling the more difficult it is to screen the light source, and the number of fittings you need in order to provide for different activities will seem excessive to anyone who has never had to tackle this problem. Nevertheless, flexibility is much needed in buildings, and the more light fittings there are the more accommodating the space will be. One way of providing light for unforeseen uses is a generous provision of fluorescent tubes, but that is not always inviting. Lighting problems need the same exacting amalgam of imagination, technical expertise and laborious checking out as other aspects of architectural design. Although daylighting has lost its key role in the initial stage of a building's design, the usefulness, flexibility and the delight of a building are no less dependent upon the technical possibilities and limitations of lighting than they ever were.

The history of electric lighting has been short and hectic. The pressures of demand and the brisk pace of trade have allowed too little time for research and development. Windows, on the other hand, have a long history during which their design has evolved at its own natural pace. From the early days of leaded panes, all the trades involved have pooled their resources to increase the area of glass, and thus the effectiveness of daylighting. The earliest window glass was spun on a rod, which produced the thick centre we call 'bottle glass'. As skill increased, a larger circle could be spun, and from this four useful panes could be cut, clear of the thick centre. These units were assembled into casements and sashes of various proportions. By the beginning of the eighteenth century the double-hung sash window provided one of the best means of natural ventilation ever devised, allowing the warm air at ceiling height to escape while cooler air entered at cill level. This excellent performer is recognized as one of the glories of eighteenth-century architecture. And as, during the century, the viable unit of glass increased in size, the builders, owners and architects who concerned themselves with daylighting managed to increase both the overall

17 QUEEN ANNE'S GATE, WESTMINSTER

These nine-paned windows, with their refined hardwood glazing bars, have replaced the sturdier mouldings of Queen Anne's day in the original box frames.
The gradual evolution of the Georgian sash window shows how, ideally, utility and elegance can edge architecture into being.

23 QUEEN ANNE'S GATE, WESTMINSTER

Replacement of the pleasingly proportioned panes by a single sheet of glass for each sash was the next step in the evolution towards lighter interiors.

size of windows and the proportion of the total area that was glass. The panes, often proportioned according to the fashionable golden section, were steadily increasing in size. The use of hardwood enabled the joiners to slim down the glazing bars, and the lamb's tongue moulding evolved – an S-shaped curve that maximized the reflection of light into the room. More light was engineered by raising ceiling and window heights, and by splaying all reveals.

The beauty that came of this highly functional fine tuning did not deter the glass makers from pursuing new methods. The invention of plate glass – more transparent and with a truer surface than the spun variety – made it possible to glaze the traditional sash with a single sheet instead of nine or twelve smaller panes. This significantly increased the amount of daylight admitted, as well as simplifying the cleaning of the windows. The new window caught on immediately, not only for new houses but to replace Georgian sashes within the existing box frames. I do not expect it escaped the notice of the owners of those elegant houses that, in throwing out the old window panes, they were spoiling the appearance of their house. In that era of oil lamps and candles, before electricity had transformed the whole pattern of life, extra daylight must have been worth any sacrifice.

Experiments with larger windows continued, unabated even by the adoption of electric lighting. Finally, in the twentieth century, the invention of float glass provided a material robust enough to make possible the concept of the glass wall. In the 1920s the desirability of maximum daylight went unquestioned. It was the era of sun-tan, sun-bathing, and sun-worship generally. The glass wall scored highly, not only because it maximized the area of glass, but because the whole of the walls at right angles to the glass wall became reflectors, bringing light deep into the interior. Architecturally, the glass wall had a much greater significance. It gave the interior of a building a new relation to the landscape outside, bringing the outdoors in, and allowing the indoor space and its activities to flow out into the garden.

Unfortunately, twentieth-century architects have been poor communicators. The public never grasped the significance of the glass wall. For one thing, electric lighting had to some extent devalued daylight. The 'picture window' stole the show. This was a large rectangle of glass, usually centrally placed in a wall. It had the advantage of being much cheaper than an entire glass wall.

BEDFORD SQUARE, LONDON
Mid eighteenth century

This is one of London's three undamaged Georgian squares. Here is the Georgian sash window in its maturity and sophistication, giving an abundance of light, control of ventilation, and a superb architecture of under-statement. Windows and panes are all the same width, their spacing a masterpiece.
These facades express the style of mid-eighteenth-century life, with a minimum of modulation and ornament. The Bedford Estate Office controlled planning, developers and builders. Thomas Leverton was the architect most concerned with the finishing.

WOBURN WALK, ST PANCRAS 1822
Architect: Thomas Cubitt

Woburn Walk – an early pedestrian shopping precinct. This brilliant design for shops, with owners living above, is still reliably based on the unit of the window pane. The shop windows rise the full storey height and span between their glass entrance doors and the solid front doors of the maisonettes above, whose windows are broad, balconied and slightly arched.

Nevertheless, it was the first window type in the entire history of windows that was not at the cutting edge of architectural thinking. The picture window did not open up the interior to the landscape outside, nor did it exploit the walls between which it was placed as mammoth light reflectors. In spite of its name, artists have never used this simplistic window to frame their landscapes, preferring mullions or an elegant grid of glazing bars to set off the natural world outside.

Although the glass wall failed to capture the domestic market, its large-scale equivalent, the curtain wall, was more successful. This lightweight membrane, made up of transparent and opaque panels, is supported by, or sometimes hung from, the building's structural frame. It allows the daylighting to be planned independently of the building's structure. By the mid twentieth century the curtain wall was accepted the world over as a normal street facade. It looks very much a part of the High-Tech, electronic, electrically-driven world of today, but, architecturally speaking, the all-glass facade was the final development of the daylight period.

WHO ARE

CHAPTER 6
WHO ARE BUILDINGS FOR?

So far we have examined the function of buildings, the complexities of getting them built, and how design can serve the purposes of a building and enhance the lives of those who live or work in it. The question of who the buildings are for extends the architectural horizon. To its owners a building can be a marketable asset, to its users their daily work place and a vital tool, to residents a shell, a garment, almost a skin. To the passer-by it is an experience.

First consider the owner. Buildings have great potential for investment. The owner will certainly be interested in the building's market value, now and in the future. If, however, he is an owner-occupier, he will have two quite distinct relationships with the building. The value of one's home depends on how well it accords with one's personal lifestyle. The difference between the owner-occupier's two views of his building corresponds to the difference between price and value.

Buildings as containers for human life fall into two classes: those for living in, and those which house an activity or a process. Let us start with the first, with dwellings.

No one could doubt that the house they live in is 'for' them – except perhaps those who live in a house so inconvenient that they assume the builder designed it solely for his own profit. That is quite likely, since speculative builders are in the business of making money. They do, however, have to sell what they build, so at least they will not repeat an unsaleable model. Nevertheless, the claim of the free marketeers, that people are free to choose the houses they live in, is not true. Most people are pressed for money and will only find a very limited choice within their distance and price range. Others are pressed for time. They have sold their house and need somewhere to move their furniture, or they are starting a new job and their children's school term is imminent. It is undoubtedly the supplier of houses who calls the tune, whether that supplier is the local council, a housing association or a building firm.

In the case of working buildings – factories, offices, schools – their value to the people who work in them may not accord with market value. As with domestic buildings, the interests of owner and occupier may be directly opposed.

It is a fair assumption that property developers build for profit; that is to say that their main interest is in a building's market and rental value. It is not to say that they do not commission works of high architectural quality. Property developers, like members of other callings, vary in calibre. The most professional among them gravitate to the best architects, and this has led to sustained working relationships that have been successful on all counts. Where collaboration has been

BUILDINGS FOR?

profitable the architect can expect further commissions and more freedom the next time round. Where the best architects are used, the interests of the building's users will be served as effectively as those of its promoters.

When industrial and commercial firms build their own premises their primary interest will usually be to accommodate a new process or plant, or to improve their image or the morale of their workforce. I should consider these buildings as being 'for' the firm.

Buildings commissioned by government departments are presumably 'for' the nation. Before the twentieth century this used to show up in monumental, sometimes pompous architecture. Nowadays such departments frequently lease their buildings from developers, who are more practised and relaxed in their choice of architects. We, the public, have benefited. Local authorities naturally build for their local community, and since the idea of community has become less nominal and more of a reality, the pretentious facades of town halls, libraries and the other facilities such authorities provide, have been succeeded by buildings more expressive of their functions. Hertfordshire's Schools Programme, which established Britain at the forefront of educational innovation, is a happy example of what I mean by enhancement. In Europe's post-war mood of creative optimism teachers no longer wanted children to sit in rows and listen to what they were told. They wanted to stimulate a more active involvement. Charles Aslin, the County Architect, collected a group of young architects who were keen to co-operate with the teachers in planning schools that could allow for new procedures. The buildings that resulted from this partnership offered spaces where a class could dissolve into a number of groups, where projects could be set up with all their clutter. These schools are a happy example of architects designing for an idea, in this case their local education authority's idea, of the way in which education could develop for the benefit of children. These inexpensive lightweight buildings enabled the authority to test and demonstrate its new ideas about the relation of a teacher to her class.

Sports halls and the various leisure buildings are also commissioned by local authorities, but people think of them as being 'for' the individual. This is all to the good. The community is, after all, made up of individuals, and communities need to be regarded possessively by their members.

Finally, there is the sense in which all buildings are for all of us, because once they are built they can last an awfully long time. 'All of us' – the public – fall into two groups: the neighbours and the passers-by. People who own neighbouring buildings have a dual interest, financial and architectural. New buildings affect property values, both by their function and their appearance, so they can affect the value of people's homes and businesses. Passers-by can include anyone alive in the world today *and in the future*. They represent the outsider's view of a building as part of a place. This view is coming to be recognized, but it is difficult for an architect to know what to do about it. One tends to think of these strangers, of unknown age and nationality, as sharing one's own attitude to buildings – but nothing could be less likely. However, buildings have a function, even in relation to casual visitors from other ages and cultures. When you arrive in a town you might look for a post office. What you require of a post office is not that it should look Georgian. More likely you want to buy a stamp without standing in a long queue. You do not want to find the ancient church shut. If the shops, too, are shut you do not want their window displays to be hidden by blinds. Ideally you want buildings to be peopled. Obviously shops have to be shut for some of the time, but if travellers are to be left at the mercy of buildings, with nothing but brick, stone, metal and glass to keep them company, they need the buildings to be viewer-friendly. This is where architecture comes in, because architecture is the zest and expertise of the designer showing through in the form and subtlety of the building.

What shows through the fabric of many buildings is the penny-pinching attitude of their owners, and the carelessness with which those buildings have been planned. Nobody wants to gaze at meanness and carelessness. The quality of architecture does not depend upon expensive materials. It does depend upon enough time being available to get the design right. The reason why we are drawn to old buildings – particularly churches – is because so many of them are rich in detailing that we can understand and admire. We can see how well a cornerstone has been shaped to turn the corner, or a gargoyle to shed the rain. These things are done well because someone took the time to consider how they should be done. That attitude did not die with the Middle Ages. The same can happen with modern buildings, only very often the time needed for careful detailing is cut in the interests of speed. If a building is to be a pleasure to contemplate, pleasure must have gone into the making of it. It does not have to be the pleasure of carving stone. If someone has given their mind to arranging the spaces and joining the components, the spaces will be inviting to linger in, and the junctions of one material with another will catch your eye because the designer has found a way of joining them that has pleased him.

To summarize, there are four ways in which people have a direct interest in a building. Those who live and work in it identify with its function. Those in the neighbouring buildings may find that it affects the value of their property, for better or worse. Those who pass by may enjoy or resent it as architecture – as may its neighbours. Its owners are also concerned with market value. Paradoxically, they are the only group for whom this may be the sole interest.

In the long run, as we can see from the property advertisements, architectural excellence can be the most valuable characteristic of all in financial terms, but it takes time to establish a consensus of architectural quality. Only people who spend their lives in architecture can spot it immediately.

It is not only the aesthetic quality of a building that takes time to assess. Flaws in the heating installation may not be immediately apparent. It takes even longer to assess the human reaction to a workplace. This is why bankers, surveyors and other denizens of the valuation world would prefer new buildings to be replicas of older ones whose characteristics are known. Yet I think even they would, in all seriousness, agree that an architect's job is to design buildings, not always to copy them.

ALTON WEST
ROEHAMPTON 1955–59
Architect: Architect to the London County Council Housing Division

The 'point blocks' of modern housing theory are not, like the towers of S. Geminiano, statements of rivalry. Initially they were experiments with the concept of streets in the air, in order to avoid covering all of the available ground with buildings so that no space remained for recreation or planting. Even a slender tower can concentrate a couple of dozen flats on the area that would be needed for four or five houses. The ground saved is then available for children, playing fields, grass or trees. On a hill-top site like Roehampton there is also the bonus of splendid views.

Architects are in a position to assess the warring interests in a building, for they work at the hub of them. They understand the relationships and feel the clash of opposition. It is the architect who takes the client's initial brief and may have a hand in broadening or altering it as the scheme takes shape. He knows how much money is invested in a building and will have an opinion as to whether the sum is adequate for the project's worth. He carries the main responsibility for its design and functioning, at least in the case of commercial and industrial buildings, whose users only exist in notional form at the design stage. In the case of speculative developments he will be the only independent representative of the users' interests. Finally, as the design solidifies, his professional integrity – or his vanity – will involve him as the representative of the wider public who will assess the finished work of architecture. He tends in any case to be the person most aware of that public because of his occupational awareness of his surroundings.

Clearly the architect cannot afford to be a passive co-ordinator, allowing the interest of the strongest party to prevail. Throughout the design period he will be doing his best to resolve the conflicts of interest in a way that excludes none of them. This is part of the constant balancing activity that is his job. It is obvious, however, that I am describing an architect of remarkable detachment. Most architects do in fact exert pressure on the side of their own preference – whether that may be function, appearance or gain.

The local planning authority is in much the same position as the architect. Ideally they, too, should be holding the balance between economic and environmental interests. They have to weigh the interests of the community they serve against those of individual applicants for planning approval, and those of the passer-by – who is an unknown quantity. Planning officers, like architects, are individuals whose values are bound to differ.

The idea that the local architecture can have significance for a wider than local audience is clearly spreading. Architecture buffs feel that they have a stake in what they see, irrespective of nationality – and of any provable principle. This consciousness is timely. The natural world is steadily being exploited by human beings. More and more of it is becoming a man-made world. It is high time that we – the human race – assumed our collective responsibility for this process.

CHAPTER 7
VERNACULAR

Acceptance of a wider than local audience – the idea that strangers have a claim to viewers' rights in any and every building – brings the whole concept of the vernacular into question. 'The vernacular' has become exceedingly popular. Is this an unconscious reaction to our dawning feeling of responsibility for the hungry half of the world, or an instinctive recoil after stretching our minds to the wider, global horizons? This much talked of vernacular is far from being a clear concept, as you can see from the bizarre outcrop of 'Executive Housing'. It is emotional rather than practical. It badly needs to be made more articulate. It is not easy to dig ideas out of the past and discover what they have to offer the future, but since the idea of vernacular seems to generate so much energy, why leave it lying around like high-voltage cable? We had far better connect it up to the structural and social realities of building design. These could do with more powerful illumination.

It is my contention that in countries of advanced technology the reality of vernacular building belongs to the past. Chambers Dictionary describes vernacular as 'native, local, endemic – especially of architecture or general style of building'. The redundancy of the vernacular is mainly a matter of weight. Durable structural materials used to be very heavy. In antiquity the slaves bore the weight; the huge cylinders of marble, for instance, for Apollo's temple at Delphi, were inched up a thousand feet above sea level and several miles inland. Before the Industrial Revolution, stone for important English buildings was sometimes shipped from across the Channel. But for your ordinary towns and villages local stone, locally grown timber, even flints grubbed up by women from ploughed land, had to suffice. Rail freight offered choice, and steel – the uniform, calculable mass-produced structural sections – opened up a whole new territory of structural thinking. The challenge to architects' imaginations was probably as important as the structural gain.

But although local materials ceased to be obligatory – the vernacular was always dictated by circumstance – air travel and the crass hand of tourism have revived a taste for it. Other people's vernacular is very appealing. When I design a building I do not feel tempted to glance at the past, but when I visit a Greek island I do find myself hoping that its inhabitants will continue to build in their traditional way – that is, the cheapest, most laborious way, the only way that was possible for their forefathers. Is this perhaps the same syndrome that makes planning legislation a suitable curb for other people's designs but quite unnecessary for one's own? Is mine in fact a ridiculous attitude, or does the vernacular play a different role at different times and in different places?

Britain has been fully industrialized for so long that, even in the remotest places, where you might expect to find the old ways and materials, you find the ubiquitous cheap bungalow or depopulated areas. In Scotland's western isles, the Highlands & Islands Board is using its tourism budget to resettle abandoned islands, but it is not building peat bothies for the new settlers. In third world countries, on the other hand, the rural patterns of construction survive, together with the poverty that caused them. Distances are often so vast that modernization can only occur at key centres.

The question of what level of technology to apply is crucial to the success of development anywhere on earth. This truth was brought to the world's notice in the 1960s by an advisor on technical aid called Fritz Schumacher. He noticed that the impressive hospitals and factories then being built sometimes failed to prime the pump of technological advance as they were intended to do. He saw that the skills needed to operate the latest machinery, or to run the sophisticated hospital, were in the end brought in from abroad, so that the coveted new

MINIMAL DWELLING
ISLAND OF SIPHNOS

With its vine and slate paved courtyard, this looks like the ideal granny flat. But note the bucket. And where is the window?

TOWN HOUSE, APOLLONIA, SIPHNOS

The roof is vital living space. The access is the ornament.

jobs did nothing to alleviate unemployment. Worst of all, expensive developments were resulting only in impossible levels of debt. When the debts became so large that the lenders were obliged to write them off, the attempt to 'catch up' ended by extinguishing the much needed source of aid.

Modern media ensure that the disadvantaged know what life *looks* like for the other half. Technology *appears* to be something you cannot have too much of. Schumacher's achievement was to replace the false concept of technology as a commodity by the understanding that it is a way of life that must slowly be learned. He managed to sow the seeds of an understanding that the appropriate technology for any task is the one that its users can understand and master for themselves. The concept he named Appropriate Technology is just as relevant to the advanced countries as to the underdeveloped. Technology is not only 'High'. Bricklaying is as truly a technology as steel fitting. Architecture is better understood if you forget about styles and think in terms of appropriate technology. Styles can be drawn, technology is for building. In our highly industrialized and electronic age it is unlikely that vernacular technologies will often be the most appropriate. In our frenetic snatching at the olde worlde we are not unlike the underdeveloped nations in their desire for technologies they have not mastered.

It is worth checking the appropriateness of our choice for every new scheme. The first move in the design of any building is the organization of space. This, in our age of multiple choice, runs in harness with the decision on what structural system to adopt: solid walling? steel frame? laminated timber? reinforced concrete? What, considering the contractors and level of skills available, is the *appropriate technology* for that particular building?

The more thoughtful level of building design that is architecture goes on to explore the implications of this choice more thoroughly in relation to the later stages of the design. The concept of appropriateness applies to every aspect of architecture, not merely the structure. It goes without saying that the spaces must be appropriate to their uses; so must the finishes, the colour, the textures and the scale. It is the paradox of this highly functional art that, as well as being exactly right for its function, a building must look appropriate. It must wear its heart on its sleeve.

The more appropriate the choice of technologies turns out to have been, the better the architect. Since the decision on building method is the underlying structure of the design, the current health – the sanity – of our architecture can be gauged by the appropriateness of the technologies in use for the different types and scales of building. We live in a period of multiple choice, yet much of the attraction that the idea of a 'vernacular' exerts today stems from a dread of sameness. Many people fear the levelling, flattening effect of an international style. Architecturally speaking, the global village is a depressing idea. We travel for new sights and sensations, not to see the repeat of our local office blocks against the backdrop of the Atlas Mountains. Modern marketing has rubbed the bloom off foodstuffs in the same way. Camembert cheese is no longer a French experience. We expect to find it, along with scores of other foreign products, every week in the supermarket. It has become one of the week's chores, not part of a holiday, still less an adventure. It is too late to relocalize food, but as far as architecture is concerned the revulsion from global uniformity could still be salutary. Uniformity could still spread of its own momentum, but if the people who talk about architecture thought more about it they could affect its course.

Air travel is an important cause, not only of our perception of this planet as one world, but of the

PADDINGTON STATION
LONDON 1850–54
Designed by
Isambard Kingdom Brunel,
Matthew Digby Wyatt
and Owen Jones

Supremely appropriate technology for the new building type, a railway terminus.

look-alike tendency of its buildings. Airports tend to look alike and for good reasons. Their requirements are the same; they were built in the same decades; they are interdependent. That is to say that most flights need two airports, not one. By the same token, the cities that act as the junction and distribution points for air travel tend to look similar, largely because the shops and hotels at both ends of the flight belong to the same groups. If air travel is a formative influence on architecture, the pattern of trade is an even stronger one.

Following all this it is a perfectly natural assumption that architecture should have international characteristics. In the 'debate' on architecture people take sides on this issue. Far better if they would think about it and try to analyse which of architecture's dimensions are international and which should be governed by local considerations.

Let us attempt to do this now. First the vital elements – the spaces. These are the three-dimensional planning of the building. Planning is closely linked to the tempering of climate. We mass rooms together to pool their warmth, or we orientate the wings of a building in a way that will catch the cooling breezes. It might be thought that modern air conditioning would make this kind of planning unnecessary, but air conditioning is a technology that has its drawbacks; first, the high cost, and second, the more sinister consequence that it puts its users at the mercy of their fuel suppliers. Some impecunious nations have escaped from the slavery of poverty only to find themselves held to ransom by the sheiks. It will always be worth giving serious thought to the vernacular methods of tempering climate before opting for the price of High Tech. For this reason I class planning as a local concern.

We have seen why the appropriate technology for structure must depend upon local considerations. Is this bringing moral considerations into architecture? I think not. The Battle of the Styles resorted to moral and religious arguments and I suspect that the same preoccupation would be found in any century one studied in depth. What is done with very large sums of money has its moral dimension built in.

As for the social dimension, it seems obvious that this must be a local matter. What a building will offer the people who use it, and how it will affect the community, must surely depend on those people and their traditions? Their aspirations, too? Aspirations are dangerous ground when discussing architecture. People tend to hanker after the stylistic image of the social group immediately above their own. The trouble is that superficialities of style make no architectural sense. Keeping up with the image of the Jones's container is not the social dimension of architecture. The social dimension is about relating local needs to local resources.

Many laymen are drawn to what they call 'the human scale' of vernacular buildings. Often this is to confuse scale with size. The pathetically small size of many vernacular dwellings was dictated by abject poverty. The human skeleton is the basis of all architectural scale. Storey heights, the dimensions of doorways and the placing of windows in relation to the eye of the standing or seated human being, are the constants to which the scale of buildings relates. Different races vary in size – the average Swede is taller than the average Japanese – but the racial differences are no greater than the differences between individuals in the same tribe. The increasing mobility of the human race and international trade in building components have established an international coinage of components and sizes. The anthropometric constant is already globally recognized.

Designers of buildings have to reckon with human dimensions, but the buildings have to be constructed with blocks, posts and panels. Some of these, doors for instance, are tied to the

D4. Designers of buildings have to reckon with human dimensions. In particular, the heights and positions of windows relate to the eyes of human beings, standing, sitting or reclining.

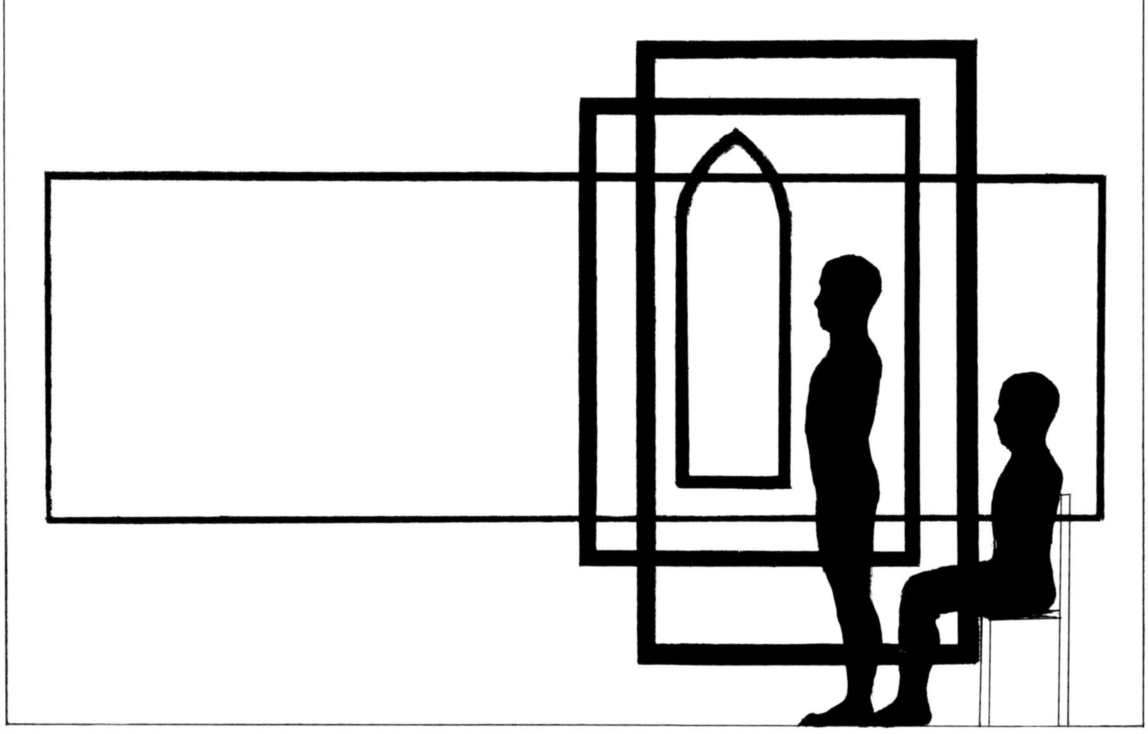

anthropometric constant. Others are designed for ease of handling: the brick for one man to lift, the panel for two to carry. Windows, whose design varies according to climate, are nevertheless a useful scaling device. The building blocks and roof trusses, the railings and balustrades, both in three dimensions and used as surface pattern, are all part of the architect's box of tricks for establishing scale.

Scale is an element of the designer's art, the outcome of his artful exploitation of technologies. Size is quite another matter. The size of the buildings that confront us is the result of the world's escalating population. That is the fact of life today and architects have to house that life and its activities.

Problems of scale that arise from the large numbers that have to be accommodated cannot be solved by borrowing methods and images from the days when numbers were smaller. We need schools which can take more than a thousand children. We need to house large numbers of families, as well as single people. It is easy to regard the enormous housing estates that we find forbidding as some stupid committee's mistake. It would be interesting to hear how the critics of disastrous schemes would set about housing all those families on urban housing lists.

The design skills exist to tame enormous buildings by means of scale. A good architect can organize the spaces needed by twelve hundred children in ways that are convincing and delightful, but large buildings will not look like small buildings. If they are to be replaced by a number of smaller buildings they will take up more land, and so will cost more, and contribute to urban sprawl. It is for these sorts of reasons that large towns cannot masquerade as small towns. Scale can relate a building to the human constant, but large buildings are units of their environment, and they set a large scale for the town or group of which they form a part.

Architecture can only enhance life as it finds it. It cannot alter the population statistics or the tendency of human beings to flock together in great cities. Mass civilization, mass education and mass culture are the most serious challenges facing architects today. Some architects have met these challenges with the sort of buildings that lighten one's heart. Stansted Airport takes all the fret out of arriving in London – not because it is in the country, but because its architect, and its financiers, have grasped the nettle and faced up to the task, providing all the services that arriving and departing passengers may need. Like Le Corbusier and Louis Kahn before him, Norman Foster is very conscious of light. If you are lucky enough to arrive at Stansted on a sunny day, you do not have to say goodbye to sunlight. It enters the building with you. The other boon is the direction finding. You can see exactly where to go, whether your direction is Scotland or Lands End. You can wheel your luggage to the appropriate railway carriage and legitimately discard the trolley. By contrast one can think of many supermarkets that have *not* been designed to eliminate fatigue. The fairytale roofline, the logo and the Mickey Mouse styling do not help with weightlifting, nor with the mental gymnastics of menu-making. It is not the *image* of High Tech that can take the drudgery out of food hauling or the fatigue out of travel, but the use of every technique available to make the best of life as we are living it.

Stansted Airport lifts the heart because its architect loves flying. This sounds naïve certainly. I say it nevertheless, because my arrival there on return from a holiday brought so vividly to my sceptical mind what Foster has said. And as I moved effortlessly from aircraft to the waiting train, all my experience of designing confirmed his statement. Foster had said that part of the joy of flying was walking straight on to the airfield where the aircraft was standing. The

S. GEMINIANO, TUSCANY
Thirteenth century

The towers were built by leading families in the town to ensure their safety and assert their relative power – very much the same role as the skyscraper plays in the business community of New York.

Stansted commission was to him a challenge to prove that all the routes, mechanisms and systems essential to the working of a modern airport could be organized in a way that did not obscure the drama of leaving one's daily round and embarking on the adventure of flight. I think he has proved it.

To design an airport tests an architect's vision on the largest scale, but I have tried to show that, on any scale, it is imagination that makes architecture – the architect's vision of life going on in the building to be. Put not your trust in the vernacular. Put it in the human mind, in a well-chosen architect.

KEEPING UP

**CHAPTER 8
PLANNING FOR CHANGE**

So far I have concentrated upon the nature of architecture, on what kind of an art it is. My message is that a building is not a heap of attractive materials but the place that has been made of them. If that place is not to restrict or impede its users, but to offer them freedom, its architect will have to summon up his own vision of the future. This habit of taking a step, however small, into the void divides architects from the rest of those who may be looking at contemporary buildings.

We all of us bring to old buildings a certain amount of knowledge. We have an idea how walls are built from playing with wooden bricks as children. We know how an arch works, even why the pointed arch supplanted the Norman. But few people know when they look at a great, colourless wall of glass, like the facade of Nicholas Grimshaw's printing house for the *Financial Times*, that the excitement of it lies in the fact that it is *hung*, and in the delicacy of the fixings. Another aid that we bring unconsciously with us to old buildings is a patina of pleasure, formed on outings and holidays, from college dining halls or choristers' voices.

The shock of the new can, like a cold plunge, turn to delight. As you stare in amazement at a new building you may begin to grasp the significance of its forms; or the shock may be your lasting reaction to that building's crudeness and insignificance. But only if you know what the design is about.

For some people curiosity is enough to make the unfamiliar exciting. Most people have to make an effort to get acquainted with new forms, to read magazines to discover what architects are thinking and what their problems are, to look at buildings, enquire about them, and go back and look again.

Architecture is a service art. A designer can simply package new ideas and conventions, or he can build a bridge that enables the present to become the future. When the motor car opened up the planet to every man and his family, no such bridge was formed. That potential agent of freedom became at the same time a nuisance. When the possibilities of concrete and stronger glass arrived, the early masters of the Modern Movement, like the builders of Christendom, did offer a vision of the world that could inspire. Unfortunately the tempo of twentieth-century life leaves little opportunity to consolidate what is new.

In this chapter I shall try to show where our architecture stands in the context of history, that is to say what kinds of change we have faced and are facing, and what challenges such changes

WITH LIFE

offer to the promoters and designers of buildings.

THE CHANGES

Buildings in our electronic and heavily serviced age are very complicated – like the human beings who occupy them. We are unlikely to find a perfect building. This is not to suggest that the faults that all buildings contain should be ignored. It is to suggest that we approach new works of architecture – or for that matter of any art – with our curiosity and powers of comprehension switched on.

What strikes many people about the architectural scene is that the present seems dislocated from the past. Yet if you compared a modern youth, with his electronic gear and motorcycle, with a youth of 1794, might you not feel the same? There have been perhaps eight generations of evolution between the two young men. We need to consider what has changed about the way human beings live, during that time, to cause the dislocation.

The winds of change that affect building appear to blow from many directions. The most obvious is building's own field of constructional techniques. There are inventions like electric lighting, that apply the discoveries of science to buildings. There are bright ideas like piped water and plumbing. And there are the products of industry, sinks for instance, or plate glass.

The contrary wind is fashion. What could be further from the mundane sphere of copper piping and electric wires? The most dramatic manifestation of fashion in the building world must surely have been the Renaissance. It did not begin with the trivialities usually thought of as fashion. It began on a high plane of excitement when Greek scholars fled westwards after the fall of Constantinople. Architecture begins with excitement and the architecture of classical Greece was something to get excited about. It was an architecture well suited to the Italian climate, less so to the humidity of northern France and England. That is where the element of fashion came in. The tide of the Renaissance continued to flow northwards, undeterred by the cold, adapting its forms to local conditions for four centuries. Towards the end of the nineteenth century the relevance of classical forms was seriously challenged in England. Augustus Welby Pugin and John Ruskin were among those who believed that Gothic was the architecture of spirituality. Thereafter classicism came more and more to be copied by hacks, its details borrowed for the decoration of machine-made products.

ALFRED RICHARDS MEDICAL RESEARCH BUILDING
UNIVERSITY OF PENNSYLVANIA 1957–64
Architect: Louis Kahn

The square block of well-lit studios and their attendant solid brick towers dramatize the relation between served and servant spaces. The three towers to the right are air intakes to a service tower containing animal rooms, lifts, stairs and toilets, all serving the groups of scientists who work in the studio block.
Kahn held that the designer must first discover the form of a building, then design the building: discovery being the scientific scrutiny of the building's purposes and needs, design the architect's personal method of transforming his ideas into solid structure.

Architectural exploration was directed towards creating an architecture suitable to the machine age, of which designers were naturally very conscious. By the 1930s the great tide of the Renaissance was on the ebb. Yet only a generation later a series of minor fashions washed classicism in again in the debased forms we meet today.

During the last two centuries some of the inventions intended to ease the lot of man – and woman – have been so popular that they have changed the world we live in. Such changes assume the proportions of cataclysm. When you are in the path of a flood you have certain options: you can take steps to save yourself; you can wait to be rescued; or you can be swept away. The option you do not have is to continue with your life unchanged. So we in our world of exponential growth have many options, more than human beings ever had before. The option we do not have is to return to the localized, horsedrawn, sparsely populated world of our forefathers. The industrial revolution was one change of cataclysmic order. A second was the exponential growth in world population, produced partly by machine-made wealth, partly by advances in medical and pharmaceutical science. The efforts of the human race to provide itself with the necessities for survival have transformed it into an avalanche of consumers. The scale and the possibilities of life have been irreversibly expanded, together with the dangers to it.

A third cataclysm changed the tempo of life. In a century and a half the practical speed of locomotion increased from the speed of the post horse to beyond the speed of sound. There were three changes of gear; first the railways and steamships, then the internal combustion engine, and most recently the jet.

A fourth cataclysm was in communications, first by cable, then radio. In retrospect it is clear that the communications media have offered much more than an increase in tempo. The simultaneity that they can produce has begun to change deep-seated attitudes. The idea of a world peopled by separate tribes has begun to give place to the perception of a single human species.

THE EFFECTS OF THESE CHANGES

If you accept that buildings are constructed to house human activities it would be absurd to expect their forms to remain unchanged by such changes as these. Can we trace the effects of these changes on building design?

Look first at industrialization. The products that appear in the builders' merchants' showrooms are avidly received by householders. People scramble for labour-saving gadgets and all the paraphernalia of 'modernization'. Even in countries where the past is revered there is a presumption that, at least in the kitchen and bathroom, modernization is obligatory. The standard modern kitchen is regarded as a social necessity, even aided at times by public grants, although many people would get a better kitchen by considering their own working methods and consulting their own taste instead of investing heavily in metal cabinets. The stress laid by advertising on the purchasing of products can be counter-productive. Gadgets and containers are only the raw materials for making a comfortable place. The products are consumed but often not digested – that is to say absorbed into the spatial and aesthetic pattern of their owners' lives.

This absorption is the design process as it applies to modern life. The owner planning her own kitchen, or the architect planning a computerized banking hall, has to select the ready-made components and then work out how they may best be arranged in the space available. The economics of industrialization has changed the design process for owners in exactly the same way as it has for architects. You can no longer leave the fitting in of components to the joiner's expertise. You need to measure the components and the space they are to occupy and work out all the joints and sequence before you buy, just as the architect must do before specifying. It is an unfortunate fact of modern life that this comes hard on the amateur.

If you do not devote time to choosing colours and what goes into your kitchen it will not come alive. If you do not decide exactly how to fill the odd gaps the place will be shoddy. In our world of plenty, selection and careful detailing are a fixed penalty – indoors and out. The smallest additions to buildings still need this care. If you cannot be bothered you will be adding to the mayhem that none of us likes to look at. These unthought-out bits of building get included in the package reviled as 'modern architecture'. They are certainly a part of modern life but they are not architecture, precisely because no one has bothered about them.

The electric wires and pipes and ducts that have so long been an essential part of our buildings took a remarkably long time to work their way through into the architecture. Houses with bathrooms do not look very different from their predecessors, and it so happened that the statutory toilet facilities of multi-storey office blocks could be fitted into their staircase towers. This may have reinforced the tacit assumption that piping and wiring should be decently hidden like our own veins and intestines. It was Louis Kahn who first stated the claim that these valuable elements surely have to architectural expression. Kahn began to talk about the 'served' and 'servant' spaces of a building. The Richards Memorial Laboratories at the University of Pennsylvania have their servant elements in the form of imposing brick towers. Kahn's insight paved the way for High Tech later to exploit the intestines themselves as a building's ornament, as we see them at the Pompidou Centre and at Lloyd's of London.

All over the world the population explosion has created a demand for more and larger buildings. The extra strength supplied by steel has been engaged in supplying them. Groups of large buildings have been steadily expanding the scale of urban building for a century now, the most challenging of them being, of course, the skyscraper. It takes a very talented architect to relate such buildings to an ancient town, and we are seeing the skyscraper, in the hands of mediocrities, playing hell with our cities. The same can be said of some of the very deep buildings that the concept of permanent artificial lighting has made possible. Architecture makes buildings comprehensible, and we have today a great volume of incomprehensible buildings. In developed and developing countries there is pressure to build schools, hospitals, houses, supermarkets and offices; and where there is pressure to build, the powerful consortia of the richer nations seem very willing to oblige.

The extraordinary acceleration of the means of transport – by land, sea and air – has had two major consequences for architecture. First, the development of rail freight, by ending the dependence upon local building materials, put an end to the necessarily regional character of architecture, and in doing so confronted architects with a greatly expanded responsibility for the character of their buildings. Secondly, and far more catastrophic, came the consequences of widespread car ownership. It was a great virtue of the railways that they knew their place. Locomotives keep to their tracks. When motor cars arrived on the scene it became clear that they had, as yet, no place. A single motor car takes up as much room as a dozen people. The roads were too narrow for these vehicles, the corners too sharp. And their parking needs have proved to be many times the area of the buildings they were supposed to serve.

It was already clear in the 1930s that cars needed a new road network in scale with their

LLOYD'S OF LONDON
1986
Architects: Richard
Rogers Partnership

Kahn's insight took root and proliferated. At Lloyd's the servant spaces and hardware are dramatized and the joy is evident. It strikes you from the first sight of gleaming steel and rococo staircases.

SEAGRAM BUILDING, NEW YORK 1958
Architects: Mies van der Rohe and Philip Johnson

Judging from the external detailing of the Seagram tower, Mies perceived better than any previous architect 'what a skyscraper wanted to be'. Seagram looks immensely heavy, immensely tall. The I-beams projecting beyond the glass face emphasize those characteristics. Seagram does not seem to refer to any previous building. It is simply itself. To those who can read architectural detailing it is a revelation, but it is the night-time image that has become accepted as an image of twentieth-century beauty.

speed. It was also plain that the towns of the future would need an entirely different structure. The motor car did, however, create its own restraining mechanism, which was planning – the legislation and the profession to operate it. This did not happen until ribbon development and the new roads had done untold damage, slicing through towns and causing undreamt of levels of noise and pollution. If we ever do reap the rewards of 'planning' they will have to be substantial.

Planning is, nevertheless, the democratic means we possess for guarding the environment. Although it is capable of formidable power it is flawed by the drawbacks of bureaucracy. Do we have the determination to tame this Leviathan? Are we capable of devising the sophisticated techniques that will be needed to make it the friend of architecture?

Planners, like architects, have to operate in the eye of the storm. They see and must assess opposing interests – profits versus amenity, long-term benefits versus short. And planners are people, torn like the rest of us by opposing needs. They have their careers to foster and their bosses to please. Some are more at home with the economic issues, some with the aesthetic. Some have an empirical turn of mind, some are legalistic. Added to this, their profession subjects them to the temptations of power, so much so that those who successfully resist temptation often over-react. As the paid servants of democracy they may also be subject to political pressures.

Planning does appear to be a very mixed blessing. Most of us welcome it to keep other people's extravagances in check, but resent it as a curb upon our own. 'The planners' are blamed for everything that is amiss with the urban environment, and because they have not solved all the problems created by the acceleration of twentieth-century life.

Planners labour under two disadvantages. They have the legal means of making a positive contribution to their district, by creative schemes on a large scale. Many planning authorities do in fact have creative policies, often concealed from the communities they serve by the jargon and deadening prose of Town Maps and reports. The snag is that creative schemes need large sums of money, and tend to be controversial. The easier side of planning is Development Control, which consists in assessing individual planning applications. This routine side of planning is easier to administer, and since the introduction of fees for applications, it could be self-financing. The result is that creative schemes tend to be shelved until they are out of date, and then quietly buried. There is nothing very creative about a planning system that is weighted towards the negative.

The planners' second disadvantage is that their masters, the elected representatives, are elected for short terms. Politicians are by definition 'realistic' rather than visionary, and tend to shy away from long-term commitments. These problems are no reason for despairing of planning, an art still in its childhood. We should be searching for ways of enabling planning to do what it was intended to do. The whole of our heavily populated, highly mechanized and accelerated world needs well-tuned planning, not merely to preserve its beauty or even to civilize it, but to ensure that it survives at all. All the functions of planning should be subordinated to its creative purpose, which is to enable human beings to enjoy life without devastating the planet.

One fault of present-day planning should not be difficult to remedy. The pioneers who designed the education for the new profession were thinking in terms of a further degree for qualified architects. In the 1960s the notion arose that planning personnel should include a wider range of skills, surveyors and geographers, lawyers and landscape architects, economists, sociologists and traffic engineers. No doubt it should, but when the expansion took place the quota of architects dropped far too low. The importance of architects in Planning Departments is not simply to ensure that there is enough aesthetic expertise, nor that architects design the buildings of which towns consist. It is because good planning must override specialist concerns and architects are non-specialists.

It was at one time expected that modern, instant communications would solve the world's traffic problems. Instead of crowding in to work on inadequate highways, people would work at home and communicate with their colleagues by screen and fax. This has happened in a small way but it has not solved the traffic problems. So far, the beneficial effects of the communications revolution have not been upon the environment but upon human consciousness. The outstanding benefit from television and radio has been in altered world attitudes to foreigners and foreignness. The age-old perception of other tribes as potential enemies is on the wane. Even in 1993 with small wars on the increase, I still discerned a dawning consciousness that all human beings are members of one tribe, and that our common habitat is in danger. Unfortunately this hopeful attitude is stalemated by the widening gap between the Haves and the Have Nots. The Haves believe that they have a right to benefits that they see as being largely due to their own efforts. Yet for the Have Nots the determination to Have can never be less than a consuming passion. Indeed, instant communications are a cause of envy that tends to conceal any good effects of global consciousness. This consciousness has not stilled ancient passions any more than steel has solved the problems of over-population. It merely plays its part in a gradual process of change.

The architectural implications of a world consciousness are, on the whole, alarming. We saw how the development of airways tends to produce an overlay of similarity. The export of architectural skills and building technology could very well do likewise, but this is not inevitable. The quality of buildings and architecture depends upon the brains and character of individuals. A single individual, in the role of client or building financier, architect or construction manager, contractor or client representative, can affect the whole spirit or tempo of a building project. At all levels – from boardroom to parish council – people with the determination to educate themselves in the realities of building construction and its implications for the aesthetics of building design are needed all over the world.

CHAPTER 9
THE DEMANDS OF FREEDOM

*LOS MANANTIALES
RESTAURANT,
XOCHIMILCO
MEXICO 1957–58
Architect: Joachim
Alvarez Ordonez
Structural engineer:
Feliz Candela*

*Felix Candela did not
originate the idea of thin
concrete shells, but he
experimented so
imaginatively with the
architectural possibilities
they offered – particularly
in the Mexican climate –
that his name is
permanently linked
with them.
The undulating roof of
Los Manantiales spans a
clear 150 feet.*

For more than a century now the range of choices confronting building designers has steadily increased. When the railways made light of the enormous weight of stone, they offered the possibility of alternatives. This severed the age-old bonds of locality. Architects were free to choose whatever materials they thought most suitable for the job in hand. And, at a humbler level, building owners could seek out the cheapest method.

I suppose the architect's situation today – with a multitude of components competing for his attention – can be described as freedom of choice. The choice is certainly wide, but he is not so much free to choose as compelled to do so. The freedom becomes even less carefree because both the trade literature and the publications needed for checking the performance of new products and methods are constantly multiplying. And the pressure on architects to ensure that no aspect of a building does fail is increasing, because the penalties for failure are becoming ever more severe.

Freedom is a condition rightly prized, but it carries with it its own responsibilities. The most demanding of these for twentieth-century architects has been the necessity to rethink the whole procedure of building design. Not only has the partnership of electric lighting and the structural frame made the central problem of traditional architecture redundant, but the only dimensional limit to the depth of a building today is the extent of the site, or any regulation that may exist on density. The designer has to analyse this amorphous building type and establish a new order of problem solving. It seems as though the strength has migrated from the architect's know-how to the structure of the buildings. This is a good analogy. Cast iron, then steel, then reinforced concrete presented a steadily expanding challenge. Each architect has been free to meet the challenge in his own way, but the freedom is immensely demanding.

In terms of creativity the most demanding of these innovations was reinforced concrete. To reap the cost benefits of the steel frame it is best to build to a rectangular grid. The thin slab, or shell, of concrete reinforced by the appropriate mesh of steel, can accommodate forms that are free in three dimensions. With metal or plywood shuttering you can build forms as complicated as any you can draw. Buildings today can absorb their stresses very easily. But can their architects?

You may well wonder why our grandfathers did not themselves design the necessary changes in design methods, and set the profession on the right path, in the first half of this century. No doubt Mies van der Rohe and his contemporaries thought that they had done so. But the profound changes they had pioneered needed a period of consolidation longer than anything the speed of twentieth-century life allows for.

In the days before building traditions were derailed by the new technologies, buildings were constrained by physical necessities, the span of timbers or the angle of light. In those days of narrower options architects could proceed with confidence. Now they no longer work in the well-charted field that Renaissance architects exploited so skilfully. Renaissance man could realign the pilasters, heighten the pediment. There are still architects practising today who think it appropriate to work in this way. Those who do not think it appropriate are, in my view, the true traditionalists, being acutely aware of time and geared to a period, two or three years ahead, when their current building will go into action. The form and rhythms of their buildings are discovered during the process of meeting the demands of the brief from the available materials, components and technologies.
This must not only be done in a way that keeps conflicting requirements in balance; it must also make it clear where the architect stands in the built dialogue of the day.

An architecture is built slowly, with difficulty,

ST MARTIN'S IN THE FIELDS, LONDON
1721–26
Architect: James Gibbs
Seen from the NATIONAL GALLERY 1832–38
Architect: William Wilkins

The wit and confidence of Gibbs's design suggest that the Renaissance vocabulary he inherited was a stimulus rather than a discipline.
The National Gallery has more the air of an academic exercise. In spite of this, and although a century divides the two buildings, they combine to form a rich backcloth to London life.
It took another hundred years for that tradition to wear thin.

as were those craft traditions to which cautious people turn for instant answers. The reason for the slow pace is that an architecture evolves building by building, that is to say in years rather than in days. Our traditions were built up over a long period, each generation taking its small step forward, as it made the familiar materials do its bidding.

Those slowly evolved traditions from a horse-drawn past can not solve all our problems because they are the traditions of muscle and scarcity. We have power-driven machinery to lift weights previously unimaginable, and produce a wealth of components. We have to work towards an architecture of power and plant, of mass production and multiple choice, that will put to good use our structural abilities and the inventions at our disposal.

It seems a reasonable enough proposition. Why then has a century gone by since architects identified the need for this new architecture, with so little achieved? Speed was to have been one of its characteristics, just as we think of it as being a characteristic of the electronic age.

It is frustrating that the tremendous acceleration of human living does not apply to the human mind, because architecture, however difficult to define, is unquestionably a matter of mind. Thought has to be applied, right from the initial concept of related spaces, to every stage of a design until the details are decided, and the information needed to enclose those spaces is complete. Though we have instant communication and computers modelled on the human brain, these still have to be programmed by the slower human prototype. The questions that arise from the new technologies of building and the new tempo of life still rely for their answers upon our unaccelerated minds.

The building process offers a good example of these two speeds at work, simultaneously but not in harmony. Drawings and Architect's Instructions can be transmitted by fax, but the fact that it takes only minutes to transfer these documents across continents does not mean that ideas will necessarily travel at that speed. Ideas have first to attract the relevant person's attention, and then to be processed at human, not electronic, speed. Moreover, drawings and instructions can only initiate constructional processes. The physical work of building has to be carried out by human beings, who are motivated by their own needs, not the building's. Even on the kind of building where the work-force is highly organized, it is not organized by the architect, but by the subcontractors who hire the men, and by a number of different trades unions. And again this organization is in the interests of the workers and employers, not of the building they are engaged upon. It is perfectly possible to interest the building work-force in the idea that makes the building architecture, but this is not done by fax or at electronic speed. It is done by the unpredictable processes that make for a meeting of minds.

The building of the Hongkong and Shanghai Bank is an example of what can be done when the electronic and the human communication systems are working in harmony. Needless to say Foster's near-impossible programme for design and construction to run concurrently depended upon full use of modern communications. While the messages flickered on the screens, architects, engineers and components criss-crossed the world's flight paths. Even so, all this could not have succeeded without an architect who was able, wherever he went, to communicate his clear vision of what was needed to the relevant group of human beings – first to the committee selecting the architect. Norman Foster Associates, who had not yet built anything higher than four storeys, who had never designed a bank, and had no experience of Hong Kong, lacked all of the stated qualifications to be considered for the job. Nevertheless, they were appointed because the committee was impressed by Foster's total engagement with the problem, his insistence upon flexibility, and by the fifty questions *he* asked *them* in answer to their request for proposals. A further test of his communicative power came in December 1984, when it appeared that the July deadline could not be met. Foster not only envisaged a Task Force, consisting of the Bank's construction co-ordinator, the Management Contractor, and representatives of his own firm and of the structural and mechanical engineers, working as an integrated team, on site for whatever hours were needed, solving problems and issuing verbal instructions. He actually inspired the eight high-powered individuals with the determination to take on this appalling task and win. The programme was not again on schedule until November 18th 1985, when it was handed over on time.

Some buildings do get built fast, but I hope I have managed to show how the organizational problems make even our power-assisted construction process a ponderous business. In spite of the fact that architecture can make an instant visual appeal, it still takes long periods of time for new influences on an architect's thinking to work their way through into his built work, and thus to influence others. New ideas can hardly ever influence buildings already under construction, and their effect on those on the drawing board is seldom profound. This means that it can take the entire design-and-build period of a project to pass on architectural ideas from mind to mind. This is why, even today, the time factor is a powerful brake on architectural evolution. It explains why the architecture intended for the twentieth century has totally failed to keep up with the building programme.

The freedom that architects have inherited ensures that they are not all travelling in the same direction. In any case, architectural evolution is not a simple journey between two points. It depends heavily upon the contribution of the most creative architects – and the strongest characters among them – at any time. There are seldom many highly creative architects, but always more than one, and their ideas are unlikely to be perfectly attuned. The less creative majority tends to group itself around the creative few. The situation is complicated by the fact that powerful personalities who are not creative at all exert an equal magnetism. The brighter young architects can distinguish between the genuine and the phoney gurus, but it is clearly a difficult matter for laymen.

Wide, and even daunting as our freedoms can appear, they have their limits. It is the enormous scope of modern technology that presents the challenge. The limits are imposed by society – by the planners, by purely conventional expectations that may exist among clients and their financial advisers, and by the scramble for status.

In Britain a confrontational relationship has established itself between architects and planners. This is sad because British architects were closely involved in framing the planning legislation in the 1940s and gave the new profession an enthusiastic welcome. Since the planning qualification was conceived as a further degree for qualified architects, the 1947 Planning Act took no account of the aesthetic aspects of design. It turned out, however, that aesthetics were frequently the main issue in deciding whether to grant planning approval. The later Acts therefore gave planners a measure of aesthetic control. In the meantime planning had, throughout the world, become a multi-disciplinary profession. University Planning Departments were admitting students with first degrees in economics, law, geography, social science and every other subject thought to have a bearing on the organization of the built environment. This achieved a desirable mix in the profession's corporate skills, but has weakened architects' confidence in its design competence. They find it inappropriate that they must accept the aesthetic judgement of planners who have not served the gruelling design apprenticeship on which a relaxed aesthetic judgement is built. It can also be humiliating for architects to have to submit their professional work for approval on exactly the same basis as members of the public, who are not only lacking in design training, but may not have the slightest interest in the subject. Obviously neither of these situations augurs well for the working of the planning system.

Many nations – and the USA is a good example – have arranged their planning laws and customs so that planners and architects accept each other's role and functions. The British situation may simply be an example of the disadvantage of being first in the field. Other nations have been able to improve upon the prototype. I think it may also stem from the interaction of a cultural quirk with Britain's rich scenic and architectural inheritance. The British Isles comprise an extraordinary range of geology, and consequently of habitat, in a very small area. The towns and villages, likewise, record their history in many contrasting materials and ways of building. The British see it as beautiful, but they have a strong tradition of philistinism alongside a great literature. The equivalent of a geological fault runs between the visual and the literary cultures in these islands – more about this in Chapter 11.

WHAT ARE

**CHAPTER 10
THE GENERAL**

The questions about building – what for? who for? who pays? – were asked in an attempt to clarify how the idea of architecture arises. Who introduces it, how do we assess and measure it? I am insistent that architecture belongs to buildings; that it does not, in spite of all the paper used in its production, belong on paper. It occurs when a certain cast of mind applies itself to the making of a building. Hitherto our sights have been on the art. Now let us consider the architect.

In examining the business of building I made it clear that a natural talent for designing buildings that can delight and command respect is not the prerogative of architects. The minority to whom it comes naturally to think in three dimensions have a head start in this game, but to reap the advantages that industry and technology offer us today, designers must be tuned in to the market place and to what is happening on building sites around the world. They must either have very powerful antennae and be prodigious readers, or work in an architectural office where they can tap in to a well-serviced library and to other people's experience.

Architects work at a disadvantage. They are generalists in a specialist world. Our culture teaches us so wholeheartedly to revere 'the specialist' in whatever field, that the architect's blatantly non-specialist function causes a certain amount of embarrassment. People wonder what exactly does he *do*? There are after all engineers to work out the precise design of every aspect of a building – structural, mechanical, electrical, acoustic – even specialists for analysing the bearing strength of the subsoil without digging a hole. Costing is the specialism of the quantity surveyor. People are left with the unsatisfactory impression that the architect provides the frills.

The reality of the job is very different. The architect is a cross between chairperson and referee, and pregnant with the embryo design into the bargain. Since the architect has to conceive the infant design she shall for the remainder of this book be female. She is always somewhere at the hub of the action, mediating or intervening between the protagonists. Her situation is ambivalent because she is both the initiator of the design and its trimmer. She must speak the languages of all the specialists, and be able to read their drawings and assess their skills and the strength of their arguments. Only she can decide when to modify a design as they advise, and when to stand firm. In Britain even her predilection for innovative design must be kept in check because it is an attitude currently distrusted here.

A building, like a human being, needs to be strong and stable, with good circulation and a healthy skin. It should be well proportioned and also adaptable. Above all it needs to amount to something more than the sum of its parts. This 'something' can not be added on at the end, for it arises from the perfect balance of all the building's attributes. This is the reason why a nonspecialist has to be in charge.

The concept of balance does not only apply

ARCHITECTS FOR?

HARDWICK HALL, DERBYSHIRE
during the 1590s
Designed by Bess of Hardwick, Countess of Shrewsbury

This great house could have been a shock to a generation accustomed to the scale of fortified manor houses or timber structures like Little Moreton Hall. Its height and uncompromising rectilinearity must have struck newcomers as astounding, even deplorable, as New York skyscrapers or the Villa Savoye did in the twentieth century.

to the components of a building, but to that building's relation with its neighbours and with the surrounding countryside. There is a strong demand in the less dynamic parts of the world for a building to 'fit in' with its neighbours. This concept can be used to deny the validity of the new. If the newcomer amounts to architecture surely it will have something to offer the neighbours as well as something to gain from them? It may complement or flatter them; it may even shock – as Hardwick Hall must have done when first it towered above the existing concept of a house, and many a masterpiece has done since. The art of building, which is in any case an adventure, is bound at the very least to be full of surprises.

The conditioning that causes us to revere specialists causes architects to suffer in the eyes of their clients. Although the client's best interests must demand a building where everything is in balance, clients are often more respectful to the specialists' dictates than to the advice of the architect, who is their natural ally. For the role of client is, like the architect's, that of a general. Does he not want a building where all the services are in harmony, with each other and with the spaces they serve, rather than one where the electrical work is outstanding but the planning poor? It seems that it is only in the army that the general can come into his own.

In recent decades the architect's traditional claim to the leadership of the building team has come into question. A cogent claim for the leadership is made for the construction manager, a role that has been very successful in shortening construction time. A shorter contract period means lower costs, which delights both client and architect. The case against the construction manager as leader of the team is that his priority has to be the smooth running of the construction *process*, while the life of the building can only begin at handover, when that process is complete. The case for the architect as leader rests upon the longer focus she has on the building, in terms of time, of its users, and of its relation to its environment. The architect's pivotal position – between the client's intentions and the complex artefact that attempts to realize them – should make her the person best equipped to keep the right balance between the peremptory demands of the contract situation and the long-term needs of future users.

The architect's broad, general view offers further advantages, beyond the ability to balance the elements of a design. Architects tend to be aware of fringe activities and of budding new sciences, like the current specialisms in the study of pollution. It is usually the architect who presses the heating engineers to consider renewable sources of heat, not the engineer who brings these methods to the notice of architect and client. Specialists tend to be cautious – which is understandable because new technologies have teething troubles that could threaten the oracular esteem in which specialists are held. The breakthrough for necessary conservation measures, like renewable heat sources, always has to wait for a generation of students to become teachers, and for *their* students to rise to positions of responsibility in their profession. An architect still needs luck, as well as competence, to make a success of installing heat pumps or wind generators.

The ranging habit of mind, tuned to the future, is the renewable power-source of architecture. Yet it is still a quality that arouses distrust. Consultants do not like it because it involves them in time-consuming research. Clients do not like it because new ideas and new technologies may not appeal to their financiers and insurers. They probably regard it as further proof of architects' regrettable failure to become specialists. This characteristic, which is architects' most important contribution to civilization, has no doubt helped to isolate them from their peers in other professions and walks of life.

CHAPTER 11
THE GAP

A comprehension gap exists between architects and other 'educated' people. The oddest thing about this gap is that the higher the education the wider it is.

I have no doubt that the fact that architects are generalists has something to do with it. In other fields the higher you climb on the education ladder the more narrowly – and profitably – you specialize. The fledgling architect leaves the university with a Master's degree, yet unspecialized to the extent that she does not even align herself firmly with either Arts or Sciences. What, say the specialists, is she trying to *be*?

No other profession hovers so tiresomely above the Arts–Science divide. Architects have no choice in the matter. They must remain unaligned because, while it is necessary for them to understand the physics of heat, light and sound, and the workings of compression and tension, their overriding responsibility is as artists. Their job is not merely to build but to produce architecture, and that, although firmly based on science, is an art.

Medicine too is a profession based on scientific knowledge which can only be practised as a skill. Buckminster Fuller used to contrast the sureness with which the medical profession had established its power base and the status of its practitioners – even general practitioners – with architects' sad lack of status. In America however this has changed. The balance of esteem between the two professions seems to have shifted in favour of architects. In Britain architects have sunk even lower. Yet when English people consult their GP they dress neatly, listen attentively to his diagnosis, and swallow any misgivings with the pills. The surgery is accepted as a staging post on the route to the Specialist, to whom patients attend with even greater reverence. Yet these prestigious doctors started off with the same handicap as architects; they were non-specialists earning their living by practising a skill.

Teachers have not done nearly so well for themselves. Primary school teachers – the GPs of their profession – likewise form the base of a pyramid whose apex is the specialist, but their standing is not nearly as high as the doctors'. Their profession has not succeeded in weaving the glamorous cocoon that protects the medical fraternity. Primary teachers foster those precious skills – reading, writing and calculating – that are necessary for acquiring all further education. The catch is that skills confer little status. General practitioners and architects exercise skills that have taken them eight years to develop. Skill simply does not exert the same magnetism as specialization. This remains a fascinating mystery, like the comprehension gap.

Infants have highly receptive eyes, so it would seem that there is some element in the advanced echelons of education that actively diminishes that receptivity. Perhaps that is putting it too strongly. It may simply be that the concept of space is not specifically included in general education. Art teachers introduce the idea of solid, three-dimensional form, but not so far as I can discover – its opposite, the concept of enclosed space that we occupy and move about in. Our relationship with this surrounding space, which is the basis of architecture, is left for children to discover and develop for themselves. In Britain, where the culture has a marked bias towards literature, at the expense of numeracy, this is to be expected. Compared with the French and Italians we are only partially sighted. It is only in relation to fashion that we take our eyes seriously. 'Pictures are very nice for children.' This puts an art that is mainly perceived by eye at a serious disadvantage.

To get the measure of this you have only to consider London's serious newspapers. Compare the space regularly allocated to book reviews – often a weekly page – the Book Supplement, Books of the Year chosen by the famous, the Christmas Books, and the endless carry on about the Booker Prize, with the occasional piece about architecture. Books, both fact and fiction, are judged to be of interest throughout the year. Architecture needs a first-class row to earn it space. Rudeness in literary criticism tends to be oblique, subtle or restrained. Buildings and their architects can expect full, frontal attack. I do not know whether to regard this lack of space for architecture as the reason for the boorishness or its outcome. In either case I presume that the connection is significant. It is also very odd, when one considers the fact that reading books is no longer an essential characteristic of the thinking person. There are clever and highly educated people around who never read for pleasure. Not everyone has a roof over their head – but we are all surrounded and confronted by buildings.

A new line of enquiry about the culture gap is raised, quite fortuitously, by the designation of the architect in the latter part of this book as female. The architectural profession has never had a high proportion of women, but is there perhaps something effeminate about the practice of architecture that divides its practitioners from the regular guys? Certainly there are two characteristics that architects and women have in common. One is low pay. Architects come low on the professional scales. The other characteristic is shared by the large female group that consists of mothers. Architects, like mothers, are prepared to work very long hours if their children+designs need them to. They are thought poorly of for not having the clout to demand overtime. The truth is that, although they are paid by their clients, architects have a personal investment in ensuring that their buildings are built precisely as designed. If this means that they have to work through the night or the weekend, most of them will do so. The fee agreement with their client does not specify hours – and the same can be said of marriage vows, or whatever may serve as an agreement between the mothers of young children and the fathers. This personal involvement with the product exposes architects to what is seen by many people today as exploitation – a problem that professions whose products are not so embarrassingly visible as buildings have been able to do something about.

Fascinating as it may be to speculate, the gap that isolates architects does need to be closed. It divides the people who promote building projects from those who possess the skills that would help them to build more effectively. It inhibits mutual confidence between designers and the constructors of those designs, and so wastes that expensive commodity, time.

All architects must be aware of this gap, even from student days. For me it became actively painful when I covered architecture for a great newspaper. Although I built up a large readership it never included the men at the news desk. Every single suggestion for coverage of buildings, or of legislation affecting their quality, had to be fought through. Curiously enough the women who took their turn at the news desk did accept architecture as a part of life and one of the Features Editors had a very sophisticated grasp of the subject. I have never discovered why those intelligent newsmen, from very varied backgrounds, could take all the rest of life in their stride – crime, politics, banking, all manner of sex, all the rest of the arts, and war – yet to a man they boggled at architecture.

In one respect the gap is wider today, the heyday of the Supermarket culture. The competitive ethos conditions us, ever more slavishly, to look for the lowest price tag and the special offer. It has always been the popular belief that in selecting a builder one should go for the lowest tender, and it is taken as one instance of the perversity of architects that they should distrust this rule. There are good reasons for doing so. Buildings, as well as being consumer goods, are opportunities for investment. They

HEVENINGHAM HALL, SUFFOLK
Architect: Sir Robert Taylor, superceded in 1780 by James Wyatt

This house and its 496 acres were offered for sale in 1993 for a guide price of £4,500,000.

can last a very long time and their value seldom vanishes overnight. We have seen that those that turn out to be classics of their period can yield spectacular profits in the long term. Secondly, cut price materials are not usually those that last the longest, and contractors who price for better design and workmanship extend the life of the building and offer savings in upkeep for as long as it stands. The fact that the lowest tender does not always result in the cheapest building is particularly true in Britain where the confrontational nature of building contracts warps the whole process. Where a North American contractor would point out an omission in the contract documents and give a price for the item omitted, his British counterpart would submit a low tender, and refer the missing item to his Claims department for inclusion as an extra.

The comprehension gap needs a special study. Sometimes it seems to be the divide between human beings who are verbally minded and those who think in pictures. That is a physical difference, born not made, but the very acceptance of its existence makes communication easier between the two. Sometimes the gap is between the specialist, very knowledgeable in his field, and the general who has to orchestrate the campaign. But broader than these physical and professional categories is the divide between those who demand a guarantee and those who, by the nature of their art, are unable to give one.

CHAPTER 12
ARCHITECT AND CLIENT

The point where the communication gap must not exist is between client and architect. Just as the quality of architecture depends upon the joints between materials and the junctions between planes, so at a more profound level it depends upon a meeting of minds between client and architect. For small buildings one person can of course fill both roles but the scale of commercial and public buildings today demands two active participants.

Building owners often fail to see what importance their role can have in the architectural outcome, because they do not understand that it is impossible to guarantee architectural success. You can not insure against aesthetic failure. You can only do your utmost to achieve success.

The market economy tends to marginalize aesthetic values. It shows us that real life has to do with money. Architects have long complained that buildings are designed by accountants, who are naturally more concerned about lettable floorspace than about functional considerations – and not at all about architecture. But although the drawing office is no place for accountants, an enterprise involving so much capital and with as many risks as building could hardly do without them. The risk of theft, the waste of valuable time, strikes, and the hazards of transport, make building look more like a pipe dream than a business venture. That clients should seek to minimize these risks is no more than common sense. What I find mysterious is that they do not make greater efforts to ensure the functional and aesthetic success of their enterprises. To fail to involve themselves in these matters is to underrate both the architect's importance and their own.

The very fact that architecture is an art should signal insecurity. Even Le Corbusier, who loved to formulate rules, admitted that 'there are no rules in art; there is success and failure'. Moreover architecture is a particularly difficult art because it needs such a wide scope of talent. The architect needs to be a powerful operator, yet she must never override the inconvenient demands of detail in the emerging design.

I stress these difficulties for two reasons. First because laymen, including building owners, are often shy of art and unaware of the kinds of problems it raises. Then, when the problems arise, they make light of them and try to push them out of sight. Some I think hope to propitiate the unknown forces of art by attention to the financial risks. My more powerful reason for introducing this is the certainty that the way to minimize the aesthetic risks of building is for the owner to assume the duties that rightly belong to him. Wherever you come across a superb building you are likely to find that there has been an impressive input of energy by, or on behalf of, its promoter.

It might be thought that, as the architect is paid to act on the owner's behalf, why should the owner also toil? In some ways it would make the design stage easier for architects if they could claim total responsibility. Throughout the design stage, however, choices have to be made, and questions about the functioning of the building answered. Many of the choices are of a kind that does not permit a compromise solution – as between formal and informal, egalitarian or hierarchic. Some of the questions are factual and easy to answer, but some concern the future users of the building, who may not yet be identifiable. These questions demand judgement and imagination, but even so include an element of guesswork. Two minds and the stimulus of dialogue can be a help. And since the building will eventually be handed over to the owner, it makes sense for him to be actively involved in shaping its future. More is hoped from the client's participation than to disarm future criticism. The aim is a dialogue that will clarify the issues, and test the validity of assumptions on which later decisions will be based.

What further duties has the building owner? First and by far the most important is to give due attention to the choice of architect. By due attention I mean all the time it needs to find the firm that the owner and his colleagues will work with happily. Alan Bullock, who was to become Founding Master of St Catherine's College, Oxford, was convinced that those choosing an architect must first see as much as possible of their candidate's work on the ground. Bullock's search took more than a year, including a six-week visit to see modern architecture in the USA as well as a visit to Denmark where the selection committee saw all Arne Jacobsen's work before meeting him. A very good way of going about their task, and a far cry from the popular belief that architects are chosen going down in the lift after the board meeting.

Building owners today offer as great a contrast in scale as do their buildings – from the gargantuan multi-national company to the individual who can just afford to commission his own small house. Let me start with the latter. Either he will know how to set about looking for an architect or he must set out to explore the architects' territory and learn their language and their ways. The obvious thing would be for him to find some new building that he likes and then discover who designed it. In Britain it is the bitter fact of the present period that many people are unable to discover a single new building that they do like – not necessarily because no such building exists, but because they are not in the habit of considering the merits of buildings. Certainly there are many people who believe that, while new building abounds, architecture is something that belongs to the past.

In fact the looker for an architect should proceed much as he would to find a practitioner in any unfamiliar field. He should go to a library or a bookstall, and consult the professional institute of the country in which he wants to build. To anyone unversed in architecture the profession's magazines and weeklies will be a big surprise. Glossies like Spain's *El Croquis* or England's *Architectural Review* use photographers who are very skilled in revealing the subtleties of building design. I should say that the world's architectural papers cater between them for every kind of reader. Architects' professional institutes vary from country to country. Some recommend architects to clients on an informal basis. The Royal Institute of British Architects claims that its staffed and organized Clients' Advisory Service, with twelve branches throughout the British Isles, is unequalled. Admittedly professional institutes cling to the convention that all of their members are equally talented and competent, but I believe a client who indicates that he knows that this is not the case will get helpful advice.

One might not expect a corporate client – a company or an institution – to have as much difficulty tapping into architectural expertise as an individual. The problem is in fact greater. Where an individual has only to satisfy his own preferences in choosing an architect, an institution has to form a human chain of communication between its own power base and all the aspects of its activity that the building will have to serve, and the smaller, but equally complex, organization within the architect's office. There is evidence to suggest that the most hopeful solution to this problem is the appointment of a single human being as the client's representative, and to delegate the choice of architect to him.

A client, professional or amateur, has a choice. He can approach the architects on his short-list by way of their buildings or the buildings by way of the architects. It is a matter of temperament. It is also a two-way process that offers the client an advantage. He is able to see the architect at work in the setting she has designed for herself surrounded by her chosen staff, whereas the only clue the architect has to the client's

ST CATHERINE'S COLLEGE, OXFORD 1964
Dining Hall
Architect: Arne Jacobsen

Surely the most classical twentieth-century building? Perhaps the most classical building in Oxford? It sings aloud in praise of light, of order, of the joy of building something worthwhile, of producing superb quality in a material that is frequently misused. We see here the precision that the Modern Movement made so much of. To see the junction of these deep beams with the cruciform columns makes one wonder why all beams are not so deep and all columns not cruciform.

To those students who respond to architecture this brilliant place must act as a dynamo and a challenge. To others it could be intimidating.

The axial approach to the West Residential block

character is the way he presents his project. The architect is in her own metier, whereas a first-time client may have little experience of building matters, and no idea what his responsibilities may entail. The fact that he has this revealing view of the architect is all to the good, because he is not buying a commodity but considering a working partnership. For good results client and architect need to be of one mind. The client should be looking for an architect whose work he admires, and whom he likes the idea of working with.

Once he has found and commissioned the architect the relationship will immediately be tested. To get the right building you need the right brief. It might be thought that the brief is a document the client hands to the architect. In the case of first-time clients this is most unlikely. Architects know what a brief needs to cover. Their experience of other briefs, of building types, and of the current state of architecture and building industry is all relevant. Many clients only commission a building once in a lifetime. Since the brief is a notional structure of the project – the skeleton on which the concept of the building has to be hung – time spent on getting it right will not be wasted. Agreeing the brief is the client's first attempt at collaboration with his chosen architect. If they find it rewarding they can proceed to the next stage with confidence.
If the client has not enjoyed it he will be wise to end the engagement at that point and look for another architect.

Next comes the design stage. The initiative now shifts from the client to architect. Since time is money and design costs salaries and overheads, the answers to the architect's questions are needed fast – and they need to be the right answers. To represent the client for a large building is a full-time job. A busy managing director is in no position to find instant answers to technical questions. His representative needs to keep up with the daily progress of the design, so that each day's questions do not take him by surprise. The reason why those pioneering postwar schools in the 1940s attracted the world's attention was that their architects were in daily contact with the education authorities, who were exploring new ways of teaching. Question and answer, requirement and drawing, were lobbed back and forth at working speed. The post of client representative is not an easy one to fill. It needs a member of the client organization who carries authority, is liked and trusted, is quick on the uptake and has some knowledge of building – ideally of architecture as well. It is worth trying to find such a paragon because it will make all the difference to the success of the building.

The problem of dragging the building process into the modern age is particularly acute in the contractual field. Traditional forms of contract have not emerged from the period when every part of a building was detailed in the architect's office. A reliable contract sum depended upon the production information being complete. In theory, once the contract is signed, the articulate, demanding client of the design stage should hibernate, leaving the architect to concentrate on ensuring that the building is built as designed. But even when this form of contract was the norm the clear break between design and construction did not reflect the realities of practice. Throughout the world the accelerating tempo of commerce and industry has forced clients, and the property developers who speculate on their needs, to frame new contractual methods that will allow design and construction to overlap. For this to happen the design team need the management skills of a contractor at a very early stage, so that full account can be taken of the constructional implications of the developing design. This enables work to start on the foundations while detailed design proceeds on the building's elements. Given a performance specification, the subcontractors collaborate in the design of these elements, and the subcontracts can be placed in sequence. In the United States these methods have succeeded in halving construction times. United by the culture of speed, the various participants in the building venture accept the leadership of a Construction Manager. The view in Britain is that this manager's independent position divides client from architect, with the result that the immediate desirability of a smooth construction operation takes precedence over the ultimate functioning and quality of the building. The British version, the Management Contractor, brought in to the design team at an early stage and given the freedom of the multi-disciplinary design office, is better placed than the Construction Manager to see that architectural values are not subordinated to constructional convenience. These experiments are on very large-scale projects. Arup Associates' Finsbury Avenue building in the City of London and the adjoining Broadgate buildings by Skidmore Owings and Merrill offer an example that testifies for the British method. A smaller scale counterpart of management contracting could well be what is needed to dismantle the confrontational atmosphere of the British building scene.

I hope I have made it clear that the function of the building owner, or his representative, demands as much self-control and judgement as any profession. Yet except in the case of property developers this is not his profession. This is why it is vital that a client should choose an architect he can get on with. During the design stage he may need to be guided by his architect, and at all stages restraint is needed to preserve the building's character. This is more often done by subtraction than by addition, by judicious pruning than by gilding the lily. Architects get plenty of practice in subordinating the parts to the whole as, day by day, they have to keep their vision of the building alive while they apply their minds to the detailed design of its parts. Most clients have not served this apprenticeship. They need to have chosen an architect they trust and are on occasion ready to follow. The way to trust your architect is to choose her with care, as you would a cooker or a dog.

People are very conscious that an architect should listen attentively to the needs and wishes of the people who will use a building. She should indeed. Not only listen to what they tell her, but be wide open to background influences that they have not mentioned for the simple reason that they are hardly conscious of them. It is less well understood that this listening should be a two-way process. Clients and the users of buildings should likewise listen to their architects, who are in a position to expand their clients' awareness of the possibilities that are open to them. Most people only know such buildings as they happen to have come across. Architects have a much more comprehensive knowledge of existing buildings and building methods. They are also aware of current thinking on design and of new ways of building. Bearing in mind a two-year period for design and construction, anyone who is not aware of the new thinking must be at least two years out of date. You need to trust your architect, not only for your peace of mind, but to get your money's worth from her fees.

I once asked a friend who had proved himself an outstandingly successful client, why there were only rooflights and no windows in his bathrooms. He replied that he too would have liked to see the views from the bathrooms but that *he never interfered with architects*. This does not mean that he had not co-operated with his architects. The point was that his house had been constructed from prefabricated, storey-height units that came in two kinds, fully glazed or solid. The eruption of small bathroom windows would have robbed this modest essay in classicism of its rhythm – and of its status as architecture. When his architect had explained this to him, Jack Pritchard had accepted that one cannot have everything, and had opted for architecture.

NATIONAL THEATRE
by day, seen from an upper-level walkway between the Queen Elizabeth Hall and the Hayward Gallery, whose rich texture and brownish weathering contrast agreeably with the uniquely polished look that Lasdun can conjure up on concrete surfaces.

NATIONAL THEATRE, LONDON 1976
at night
Architect: Denys Lasdun & Partners

As its architect describes it, the building is 'a response away from isolated monuments and towards an architecture without facades but with layers of building, like geological strata, connected in such a way that they flow into the riverscape'. Surrounding the three enclosed auditoria and their attendant towers, extrovert foyers welcome their audiences.

Looking up from ground-floor level, the cellular structure supporting the floor above is the building's ornament – a pattern that unifies the huge complex of theatres, foyers, restaurants and their servicing.

WHOSE IS THE

**CHAPTER 13
OF ONE MIND**

The relation between architect and architecture is not as clear as seems obvious. It is in buildings that architecture occurs – but not in all buildings. It occurs in solid, inanimate structures. What is it that creates a personality from sand and cement and ironmongery? This entity which is instantly recognizable is the result of the way it was designed. It comes from the mind that designed the building.

Whose mind was that? The mind of the architect. I have mentioned that the gift of enclosing spaces, of being able to regiment panes of glass in a way that produces a pleasing sash window, or making the right instant decision on site, is not confined to qualified architects. It may belong to the joiner's apprentice or the client's wife. For large buildings 'the architect' will be a sizeable team. It may be obvious who is leading this team or it may not. There may be constant and bitter arguments, but it must be that the team is fundamentally of one mind, or that there is one strong will that prevails. A further complication is that the factory-made components are the products of quite other minds. Nevertheless the component will have been chosen because the building's architect was of one mind with its designer.

To unpractised viewers the hard mass of unfamiliar architecture can seem unforthcoming, even grim. It may seem less so if they can forget the carriage lamps and gargoyles of the clinging past – or of Disneyland – and try to discover what the building wants to be, what it has to say about the future.

Different buildings and different periods of architecture tell different aspects of their story. As Gothic matured and found ways of letting in more light, it expressed ever more accurately the paths by which the huge loads were brought safely to earth. In Elizabethan times the assumption was that the inhabitants of any building would need all the daylight they could get. Facades became a lattice of glazed panels, revealing this intention as clearly as they illuminated the working surfaces of the interior. It is the candour of that architecture that Sir Henry Wotton expressed in his definition, and that candour is the reason why 'well building' was, in his time, identical with architecture. To us 'well built' only means soundly constructed and capable of keeping out the rain; it no longer means delightful.

Nowadays the delight of turning a thought into a solid, of getting the details right, occurs mostly in the architect's office. In Wotton's day the link between the designer and the finished building was furnished by the men who chiselled away on site. If they thought they could improve the detail they were working on they were in a position to do so, or at least they could speak their mind to the architect or master mason. Today the link

RESPONSIBILITY?

between designer and building is an enormous pile of contract documents. Factory-made components, packed, insured and transported great distances to their site, do not lend themselves to modification. This causes the builder to identify with the managerial operation, while the architect is increasingly stuck with its effects.

A similar cleavage exists between the architect and her consultants. Positive action has been taken to change this very wasteful situation by architects, engineers and surveyors who have established themselves in multi-disciplinary practices. It is an extraordinary experience to exchange the formalities of professional protocol for the awareness that all of the varied skills and expertise needed to build and service a sophisticated building are with you, ready to hand, under the same roof. The potential of the situation releases seemingly boundless energy – exactly what is needed to animate design work.

All over the world the processes of building are changing in ways that do not apply to the human beings the buildings are for, nor to the laws that still apply to building. I think that the necessity confronting architects – to redesign their profession and its working methods at the same time as they design their buildings – is a factor that helps to isolate them from other professions. It is a task that can prove overwhelming to any but the most creative architects, and there are never enough of these.

Architects are aware of this awkward fact but we do not publicize it, which is to my mind a mistake. American architects were much bothered about it in the 1950s. 'Architecture is word poor' is how Saarinen put it, exhorting his contemporaries to add to the vocabulary of the emerging work. Creativeness cannot be stepped up at will, but inventiveness can, and the immediate results of Saarinen's directive were not good.

The rarity of creative genius is one of the factors that makes the development of architecture such a slow business. When creativity of a high order does appear it is instantly, and astonishingly widely, recognized. New ideas appear in built form, often in parts of the world where you would not expect to find them, as one architect's creativity acts as yeast to the less creative, who can nevertheless recognize it when they see it.

Creativity is not only a rare gift but often a short-lived one. There are artists in every medium whose most creative period is over by the time they are thirty. This matters less in architecture than in other arts because architects need to work in groups, to include a wide enough spread of knowledge. When a firm needs a new assistant or partner it can renew its creativity if

1 FINSBURY AVENUE, LONDON 1984
Architects, engineers and quantity surveyors:
Arup Associates

The house on the facing page is timber-framed. In 1666 the Fire of London called attention to the superior fire resistance of brickwork and masonry. Framed structures only returned to cities with the iron, steel and concrete technologies. With them the horizontal window returned and larger units of glass appeared.

1 Finsbury Avenue was designed at a time when windowless buildings with permanent artificial lighting had been found wanting. This building has daylighting on all its fronts and the central atrium, but it is not naturally ventilated. Architecture always depended on balance. As our material wealth and understanding increase, so does the number of factors that have to be kept in balance. Daylighting is one. Heating, cooling, lighting and ventilation are all interdependent. All their hardware, pipes and wires take up space and have their natural paths, so they should take their part in shaping the building.

All these services have two levels of costing, which must be weighed against each other, the one-off installation cost and the recurring running costs. All this, and insulation too, must today be set against the need to conserve energy. How much of all this can be read on the building's face? The decision to maximize daylight is there, and the sunscreens to control solar gain. The plane trees and plants tell of a care for the quality of the air and surroundings. The nub of this architecture is its directness. What is there is what is needed. The creative stimulus is in manipulating space and light, heights, levels and temperature, to produce a place not only comfortable but elating.

SURTEES HOUSE, NEWCASTLE UPON TYNE
Mid seventeenth century

No one blames seventeenth-century buildings for being functional. Those who would not look for beauty in the masterpiece on the opposite page frankly enjoy the light shining on the glossy lattice of Surtees' windows, and the rows of homely beam ends that oversail the storey below, to gain the maximum possible floor space. Yet the seventeenth century and the modern designers were seeking daylight for the same good reasons – because it was the cheapest and the sanest thing to do. The northerner must have enjoyed making his commodious residence the best-lit house on the quayside, while Arup Associates took a professional pride in designing to the best standards of the day and enjoyed replacing a jaded area on the edge of the City of London with an attractive and efficient workplace.

it knows where to look for it. The extraordinary duration of Le Corbusier's ascendancy owed much, I suspect, to the longevity of his creative period.

One device that architects have found for concealing a lack of creativity is to sprinkle a building with references to other buildings and past styles. It appears that any reference will do. The choice does not seem to have much to do with the purposes of the building that is being sprinkled. This is a game played on architectural ground, and it is part of a serious search for architectural bearings, but it is not architecture. 'References' and symbols belong to the world of semantics, where many architectural critics live. Architecture originates in the architect's response to the building she is designing – response both in broad terms of significance and in solutions to the building's technical problems, at every scale. This kind of response is generated by the excitement of converting ideas and calculations into the tangible definition of space.

Another device is to substitute graphics for architecture, using a building's surfaces as billboards. This is a current weakness of American architecture, but the example that springs to my mind is a London building by Terry Farrell originally designed for TVam. This is a jolly container, and very relevant to the activity it houses, but its dramatic discrepancies in scale are no more than amusing. It provokes no shiver of excitement. What its exterior expresses about the glitzy transience of viewing is hung on the building as a label, rather than built into its rhythms and textures.

All the ists – Post Modern, Neo Classical, Neo Rational and the rest – are fishing around in architectural waters for a mooring, to which they can attach a flag. Classicism appears a very respectable flag indeed, only when did respectability have anything to do with art? You fish because you need to eat and offices eat up money. A flag with a name attached leads to talk, which is a good advertisement and leads to clients.

A building that is a work of art and can speak for itself is, however, an incomparably better advertisement. Unfortunately the firms with the ability to make a building speak for itself are far outnumbered by the fishers around, who have not found their true direction. Both architects and laymen are trying to find their way, the architects through a galaxy of choices, the laymen trying to make sense of what they see. In this they have trouble because much of it is not sensible. There is big money to be made today by wrapping buildings in nostalgic facades, and this is precisely the message such buildings carry.

Those architects who find their inspiration in the unexplored possibilities of their times are the ones who give life to architecture. Louis Kahn and his contemporaries were excited by a vision of vertebrate buildings with piped digestive systems and electric nerves. Today the most radical challenge to the form of buildings is the need to conserve energy. For half a century farsighted individuals have been aware that it is not possible to sustain exponential and population growth indefinitely on our finite planet. Architects, engineers, many in the construction industry, and government departments who legislate for construction, have done their best to bring the need to move to sustainable sources of heat and power to the public's notice. The idea has made astonishingly little headway against the creed of monetarism and short-term accounting. Fortunately small-scale experiments in designing for passive solar gain, heat pumps and other sustainable methods have been carried out by architects, developers and by government departments, during this happy go lucky period. If the world does finally opt for sustainability, the results of such experiments will point the way forward.

The minds at the cutting edge are never popular, particularly in our present period, when

ST GÖRAN'S HOSPITAL RESTAURANT, STOCKHOLM 1968
Architect: Ralph Erskine

This building speaks for itself most eloquently – by its own pattern of daylighting, by the varying roof pitch, by the simple but arresting metal junctions for the timbers. Look at the head and foot of the posts that support the roof beams. And the depth of the beams, supported by the slenderest of posts. It is a surprise too to see the ceiling lined with random boards. It is all a surprise, and the pleasure the designers took in surprising us comes through.

LYCEE ALBERT CAMUS, FREJUS, FRANCE 1993
Architects: Sir Norman Foster and Partners

A very traditional sophisticated building. The aim -- to provide 1,000 learners and teachers with a comfortable environment through the fierce contrasts of the Mediterranean climate, and to do it on a fixed budget in the shortest possible time.
The means -- a linear form to the building and a repetitive concrete frame to lower costs and construction time; maximum use of passive systems of heating, cooling and ventilation, restricting mechanical means to such areas as kitchens, laboratories and the covered space above the concrete roof vaults provided for blown air.
A lofty 'street' between two-storey terraces of classrooms creates the social focus of the school. It also forms a solar chimney, in the Arabic tradition, to enhance through ventilation. Heavy structural concrete absorbs internal heat to slow down temperature change. Fully glazed external walls maximize daylighting, while their metal sun shades prevent solar gain; they also create shady outdoor teaching space.
The result: a contract figure 11 per cent below budget and a powerful new image in branching steel.

buildings are likely to be very large. If the shock of the new is not delightful there is an instinct to look away – to the garish, the frivolous, or the familiar. The past can indeed look appealing, but we tend to deceive ourselves about its excellence. We forget that most of the buildings that have survived are those of exceptional quality, or with a particular historical association. They were judged worth preserving, and they were the ones that worked well. Then there is the allure of natural materials. In the days when all the buildings in a stone region were built in local stone they naturally looked well in the landscape. Their colour was harmonious and the scale was then small enough for a village to focus the landscape, rather than eliminate it. People today yearn for these nostalgic materials, yet they were originally used because they were the only materials available. I have heard people enthuse about the warmth of 'thick stone walls', not understanding that stone walls were thick because stone has such poor insulation capacity. Architects need to be wary of nostalgia for the same reason that a motorist should be wary of looking over his shoulder while driving a car.

I like the driving metaphor – the sharp focus, shifting, adapting and alert to what may lie ahead. Anyone anxious to have their say about what direction architecture should take would do well to adopt this attitude.

CHAPTER 14
FOR BETTER OR WORSE?

Enclosing space costs money, so it is not done without a specific purpose. The purpose may be wholly aesthetic – a garden or a vista – but it is usually a building, that is to say a container for some aspect of living. It may be a house or a stack of offices, a shopping arcade or a factory, a nursery school or a university, a prison or a crematorium. These spaces may be enclosed in an entirely practical way. They may be warm, watertight and impeccably built, but this as we know does not amount to architecture. Think of architecture as the building's voice. When the designer has the skill she can make the inanimate structure speak for itself.

Architecture is the art of making the sense and sensibility of a design evident in three-dimensional form. By sense I mean the functional planning, by sensibility the appropriate form for the intention. Some buildings are notable for their geometry, some for their proportions, some for a new constructional idea, others for a fine facade. But even when these highlights occur the fact of any work of architecture is that its many facets cohere into a whole. You see a beautiful facade but you think 'what a fine building'. If you react only to the facade I believe that the architect has failed.

A Bill of Quantities lists every item in a building, fixings and all, and their number is staggering. Nevertheless some architects manage to transform this pile of chaos into a coherent place. How do they do it?

I believe that this feat, which is architecture, is the result of their commitment to an idea. The sights of the architectural team are fixed, not on a catalogue of components, but upon their concept of the whole building, occupied and working. The design is bound to entail a long and tedious haul, fraught with disappointments and with arguments that result in compromises. Every item that is finally selected replaces faith with fact. With every decision, large or small, the building gains in reality, and the commitment weighs less heavily on the architects. It is this feat of sustaining the idea that gives a building the unity I describe as personality. It is this that ensures that the handrails, grilles and fittings, and the finishes on wood, metal and concrete, will eventually be recognizable parts of that particular building, or as the work of that architect. These details will relate to the spaces, and the structure that defines them, as skin does to bone.

This living quality, akin to personality, is architecture. It is there because its designer had a clear idea of the life that would go on in the building, and was bent on making it a place that would not only serve that purpose, but would go beyond that to express the spirit of the undertaking. Success in doing this is the outcome of the steady commitment I have described, but the long plod does not ensure success. There has to be the talent to find the right form, and even those who have the talent are not successful every time.

Some architecture has a particularly eye-catching quality. This lively look comes from its designer's consciousness of light, and her skill in using it to reveal the building as well as to light the activities it houses. The architect angles the building and models its outer casing to allow the play of daylight to show the subtlety of its form. The placing and proportions of the windows are vital to the functioning of the building, and the profiling of their reveals bounces light further into the interior. All this has been part of architectural tradition throughout recorded time.

Although daylight no longer occupies the pivotal position it once held in the design process, light, from whatever source, is still as crucial an element as it ever was. This is because architecture is mainly perceived by eye. It is through our eyes that all sighted people use buildings and enjoy architecture. Whether or not a lighting consultant is employed, lighting remains one of the architect's primary

THE SULEYMAN MOSQUE, ISTANBUL 1550
Architect: Koca Sinan

'A building notable for its geometry.'

The intricate assemblage of forms massed around the great central spaces of this mosque is a faithful expression of all the spaces within. This is the first Turkish mosque to achieve such a feat of architecture. The arches in the foreground appear to set the majestic scale of the enterprise. The clustered towers, domes and minarets express exaltation.

responsibilities – as important as function – because appearance is not superficial to architecture but organic, as an animal skin is to bone. The planning of a building controls the way we move about it, but its architectural impact, both mental and physical, is by courtesy of the natural and artificial lighting.

Take a factory as an example. Accountants will judge it by its output, and the demand that exists for its products, but where the figures record success, it is a part of the architectural success, since productivity was the purpose of the exercise. There are other aspects of architecture that do not show up in the accounts, because they can only be perceived by the senses. For the workforce, the factory shapes and colours the day. For the passer-by it is an experience. For the neighbours it is a part of the environment. Its design can enhance or debase any of these relationships.

Buildings can add glamour to the lives of their users, or the passers-by; or they can do the opposite. They can make their inhabitants spend the day wishing they were somewhere else, or the passers-by exclude them from their consciousness. These experiences are powerful and go deep into the unconscious. They are perceived by eye and ear and by the senses of smell and touch, working together in a complex system. Nevertheless the *main* organ of architectural perception is the eye, and this is why I keep returning to the importance of light in considering what architecture has to offer in the spheres of utility and experience.

A new building takes over an area of the planet's surface and redesigns its space, its form and its whole meaning. The site may be a primeval meadow or some such marvel, a bombed site that has become a tip, or anything between those extremes. When we build we can replace dreary by dreary, workmanlike by cheap and nasty, or stagnation by hope. Or we can of course replace like with like.

In the three and a half centuries since Sir Henry Wotton defined 'well building' the human race has effected a takeover of the earth's surface, piecemeal and unplanned. The impact of architecture and nonarchitecture has become an immeasurably more serious matter. It is always rewarding to sit back and discuss exactly what makes a building delightful, but I believe that our time is unique and has a different priority. This is the moment for everyone involved in architecture and all those who have a feeling for it, to decide what responsibility they, personally, are equipped to exercise for the built environment. The reason why we hear so much about architecture these days is that the urgency of the subject has begun to dawn on a widening public. The strident talk is the result of an uncomfortable pricking of responsibility.

I agree wholeheartedly with the dissatisfied public that it does have some kind of responsibility for what is built, and that architects do hold the major responsibility for the design of buildings. However, the quality of the arguments about architecture suggests that the serious carers about this art do not understand its nature well enough to be of much use to it. What people usually know about the buildings they admire is their date and 'style'. Few people feel the need to find out why one style succeeded the one before. We tend to look back across the centuries in a kind of dream, not in the spirit of practical curiosity that the subject demands.

We all seem to agree that it is good for architecture to be talked about. What I hear and read, however, does not seem to be about the realities of architecture. It is as though a book reviewer concentrated his attention on the jacket, and never got round to considering the book inside it.

Anyone who has followed my argument so far will know that I think that people should explore what lies behind the facades of buildings. And I hope I have convinced some of those who think

NEUE STAATSGALERIE, STUTTGART 1984
Architects: James Stirling, Michael Wilford and Associates

Geometry does not only exist in regular forms -- the cube, cylinder or pyramid. The Staatsgalerie is a formidable amalgam of the regular and the free, classic and Pop. It is not left entirely to the exhibits to remind, challenge and stimulate the viewers. Nevertheless, the stature of the building was established by the initial decision to terrace the hillside and present the museum and its contents by a series of structured routes through its ascending levels and covered and open spaces. Its integrity is founded in James Stirling's early and profound identification with the Modern Movement. The building's power seems to lie in those contrasting geometries emerging from the hillside, whose impact is both instant and lasting.

architects are not shaping up to their task, that we are living in a period when experiments have to be made. It is in the nature of experiments that some succeed while others fail.

It is time for all of us – architects, building owners, and everyone else who thinks about architecture – to consider where our own responsibility lies. I have myself listened to the current discussion with increasing dismay. Eventually I decided that, as an architect trained in the more generous climate of the Modern Movement, my own role was to draw attention to those aspects of architecture that were *not* being discussed.

Architects take a lot of flak these days. They alone are often held responsible for the state of the urban environment, although it is in the nature of their calling that, except in designing their own houses, they are never free to act independently. An architect designs to accommodate some form of human activity – education, commerce, transport or what you will – so she is always tied in to the financial system responsible for that sector. It may be that the strength of feeling aroused when an architect is censured is itself a sign that the public feels in some obscure way responsible. Architects may deserve criticism but it must be said that they deserve better informed criticism than they receive. No other profession has such a rigorous training in facing up to its critics and learning from them. Their student designs are not marked by their tutors in the privacy of their studies. They are hung up and criticized in public by a jury composed of the teaching staff and others, architects or not, invited by their Year Master. The author has to present her scheme, receive the jury's views, and defend the design in the presence of any students, staff and *members of the public* who care to attend. This process, repeated over a period of five years, tends to strengthen students' sense of responsibility, and rightly, for an architect is without doubt responsible for producing buildings of architectural quality at the same time as ensuring that they are finished on time and within the budget figure. Most architects know that the aesthetic and managerial functions belong together in one professional package. But in financial circles, in boardrooms, where clients are often to be found, and in the general mental outlook of our world, a distinction is assumed to exist. This presents architects with a temptation that can work in two ways.

Some close ranks against the values of the market place and identify with the aesthetic side of their job at the expense of their programming and budgeting functions. Others conceal their aesthetic sensibilities behind a sharp image of accountability. This is why it would be a great benefit to architecture if all the groups who bear some kind of responsibility for it were to be identified, and the extent of their responsibility defined. If the total responsibility does not belong to the architectural profession the public should know how it should rightly be distributed. If the other groups were to assume their share of responsibility, it seems likely that architects would measure up more successfully to theirs.

Building owners often underrate the contribution that they could make to the design of their buildings. The blow by blow account in Chapter 12 of the way responsibility should be lobbed back and forth between client and architect may alarm some potential clients while inspiring others. It makes it easy to understand why all clients are not prepared to assume what architects see as their proper role. Indeed some who have played their part in making an outstanding success of one building have refused outright to undertake the task again. This should not matter if they are prepared to take the trouble to delegate the duties.

A more usual image of the building owner is as the man who holds the purse strings. Some clients may hold them for a time but, except in

CHISWICK HOUSE
Begun in 1725
Architect: Lord Burlington

Notable for its scale, proportions and geometry, the most striking quality of this building is its oneness, the sense that here is something that has been done exactly right.
Lord Burlington designed this building as a temple embodying his ideas on architecture and as a repository for his collection of paintings, which may well account for the single-mindedness of the design.

the case of very small buildings, these strings are generally controlled by financial backers. Building costs are big money. Their financial underpinning often depends upon a complex web that extends more than nation-wide. The arcane world of building finance exerts an influence on architecture, often by default.

Financiers exert this influence in two ways, that may not be clear to themselves any more than to the public. It may seem obvious that the budget figure can affect the form a building takes and the materials used, but cost does not have a direct relationship with *architectural* quality. A tight budget presents the architects with a challenge that can stimulate their performance. The quality of architecture depends not upon cost but upon the ability of the architect.

The decision most likely to affect the architectural quality of a building is the choice of architect. The way in which the building's financiers affect this choice is often indirect. It can work rather as censorship works. Authors anticipate the censor's known or suspected prejudices in order to avoid trouble. Building owners, likewise, may choose their architects for qualities they believe will find favour with their financial backers – that is to say status, or a reputation for finishing on time and within the budget. Status often turns out to be a poor guide, but the real objection to this method of selection is that it relieves both the owner and his banker of their proper responsibilities. An important decision will have been taken by default.

The second way in which finance shapes architecture is more direct but equally damaging. Control of the flow of money sounds like the kind of thing financial institutions exist for. Cuts may have to be made during a building programme. It is the timing that is so important. If adjustments have to be made to the budget it is essential that they are made before the design has jelled. The slowness of the design process is often a source of frustration to the financiers of buildings.

It could often be employed by them in more accurate forecasting of possible fluctuations in their money supply. Since architecture is the result of delicate balancing and adjustment, budget changes during the design stage are acceptable as part of the day's work. It is the cuts announced during construction that make a nonsense of the plan and destroy the integrity upon which a building's architectural impact depends. This integrity can exist at any cost level, but *it has to be designed*. It can be impossible to restore it if accommodation is cut after the structural frame is completed, or when all the subcontracts are let. The most frequent defence when buildings are criticized is that they had to be radically changed during construction.

Buildings are major casualties to the wavy nature of 'advanced' economies. Modern buildings, like the higher vertebrates they increasingly resemble, need a long period of gestation, to allow their designers to explore inviting technological possibilities, sound out world markets, and weigh requirements against costs. The crop of amputations imposed upon buildings by each recession makes a nonsense of careful planning and fine architectural balance. The irony is that the severest losses are to the savings that conscientious design and ingenious methods of construction were to have achieved. The pruning of buildings under construction leaves them, unlike fruit trees, permanently maimed. The cost-effective action that the built environment needs from its financiers is that they devise a gearing mechanism between the known requirements of ongoing building projects and the bumpy rhythms of their sources of finance.

Bankers may deny that they have any responsibility to architecture but it is hard to see how building societies, property developers or those who allocate grant aid could do so. The fact remains that financial decisions – or absence of decision – do exert a strong and continuing pressure on architecture in the ways I have described. In the matter of choosing architects, the situation would be put right by the financiers' acknowledging and assuming their responsibility to state any opinion they may hold, or to hand over the task to the building owner. If bankers discussed the choice of architect with their clients the preferences attributed to them would at least be theirs. The architects chosen by the Directors of the Hongkong Bank and Lloyd's of London suggest that the money men are far more adventurous and imaginative in their architectural thinking than is commonly supposed.

Finance is undoubtedly the most important sector, after the architectural profession, to assume responsibility for the architectural consequences of its decisions. One can see why this responsibility may be unattractive to highly numerate people, because the results are uncertain. But surely not more hazardous than the stock market?

How is the arcane sector to be persuaded to assume its burden? By its clients, the building owners, and by tax payers and shareholders. I mentioned earlier some tedious responsibilities lying in wait for shareholders, and the special need there is in Britain for an influx of architecture lovers to local government. Planning has immense creative possibilities that have hardly been tapped – nor ever will be unless the architectural passions that have been roused can be harnessed. Not only the creative possibilities, but the nagging processes of development control need the services of elected representatives to whom the environment is important.

Not everyone is a shareholder – nor pays taxes – but everyone in a democracy is entitled to complain. Any citizen has the right to raise hell about the design of public buildings or Bills working their way through Parliament. We all have the right to ask questions of those who we pay to answer them.

Responsibility is not however confined to those with the talents for public life. All those individuals who have helped to turn the spotlight onto architecture's shortcomings, and those who have thrown courtesy to the winds and created mayhem for architects, have a responsibility to face the difficult questions they have raised. I am not suggesting they can answer questions that baffle entire professions, only that they should stay with the subject that interests them. They would be more help to architecture if they were better informed, if for instance they became regular readers of an architectural paper, and tested their theories against every contemporary building they came across.

This applies particularly to those people who are devoted to the architecture of some past epoch. Their knowledge of that period usually puts the scholarship of practising architects to shame. If those enthusiasts could manage to transfer their zest for the monastic or princely cultures to the purposes for which we build today, and to the financial, human and technological resources at architects' disposal, they might provide architecture with the informed, perceptive public it lacks and so sorely needs.

In religion we are urged to look to the health of our own soul. In architecture too it can be sadly instructive to look at what we do, semi-consciously, to our own buildings. When we decide to add a garage to our house do we hire an architect and instruct her to design one in accordance with our stated opinions? Or do we order the cheapest prefab, without any thought at all? When we add a bathroom do we run the plumbing neatly in ducts or let it spew out all over what was once a facade? When we replace existing windows with a type designed to discourage burglars, do we consider how they will look from the house opposite?

It is not customary to think of these efforts to keep up with life as minor forays into architectural design, but this is what they could be – and in the

THE ECONOMIST BUILDINGS
LONDON 1958
Architects: Alison and Peter Smithson
Contractor: Sir Robert McAlpine & Sons

These buildings are the product of two remarkable minds, one scholarly, one organizational. Their client said of them at the opening of the buildings: 'We met them six years ago with trepidation, and take leave of them now with affection and awe.'
Gordon Cullen wrote in The Architectural Review: *'The only way we can humanize the environment is to discover how it falls apart so that we can get inside the synthesis.'*
This may have been the thinking that caused the new premises for Martin's Bank, The Economist and their elegant neighbour, Boodle's Club, to take the form of three towers and an extension to Boodle's flank, held together by the plaza which divides them, and by the meeting of planes and the joints between materials.
Routes and views through the St James's hinterland, opened up by the plaza, integrate the newcomers with the neighbourhood and its smaller scale. Meanwhile The Economist tower proclaims its presence in the Westminster skyline and so reaches out to a wider world.
The architects' solemn attention to detailing was reciprocated by excellence on the builders' part.
Portland stone is London's traditional building material. While dressing their functional concrete-glass-metal buildings in the named product, the Smithsons selected Roach bed Portland – a material that can delight every passer-by, from toddler to connoisseur, with its age-old, seaside rusticity.

case of people who habitually criticize architects it is what they should be. A single garage is a particularly difficult building type to design gracefully, a test of any architect's skill. These minor works are the points at which many people's commitment to architecture is tested. It is the point where those people who want the buildings around them to be architecture can try their theories in practice, and learn whether they themselves possess any design skills.

Architecture cannot exist in theory. It sparks into life at the interface between mind and matter, where a designing mind engages with the solid problems of the building site. Building can become architecture when that mind is capable of seeing the functional problems in terms of geometry, and the geometry in terms of how it can be built. In this art the relation between theory and practice is as delicate as the relation between mind and body, and is crucial.

Architecture can only be practised in three dimensions, and at considerable cost, but responsibility is a form of practice that is open to anyone. To those, that is, who are prepared to exert themselves, to look, to listen and to learn.

The significant thing about the times we are living in is that our species shows signs of assuming responsibility for its native planet. People are also becoming aware that buildings are not just individual incidents on the earth's surface; that we had better look at them as part of an avalanche that threatens to engulf the earth itself. This concept invests everything that is built with a new importance because buildings are the positive, creative component in the haphazard tide of which the avalanche is composed. Its other components are waste materials, some poisonous, some merely squalid or unwelcome. It is becoming clear, from the heated arguments already occurring about the importing and exporting of waste, that a world strategy is going to be needed to balance the positive and negative elements of the earth's new man-made surface.

There may be a time ahead when the question of what is to be built and what not – and of who is to decide – may override our preoccupation with quality. Meanwhile, all the talk and the strife about architecture is greatly to be welcomed as the burgeoning in human beings of a sense of our responsibility for a future.

PHOTOGRAPHER or SOURCE
Subject identified by page number

4 Conway Library, Courtauld Institute of Art;
5 Wolf Dieter Gericke; 11 James Austin; 18, 19,
John Donat; 24 Eric de Maré*; 25 *Architects'
Journal*; 27 Eric de Maré; 32 *Architects' Journal;*
33 Tony Mann; 34, 36 *Architects' Journal*;
37 Arup Associates; 39 Country Life;
40, 41 Greater London Photograph Library;
42 John Donat; 43 Nation Buildings Record;
47 Greater London Photograph Library; 49 Diana
Rowntree; 51 Eric de Maré; 55 Prudence Bliss;
58 Alison and Peter Smithson; 61 Martin Charles;
62 *Architects' Journal*; 64 British Cement
Association Library; 66 Eric de Maré;
71 *Architects' Journal*; 75 Knight Frank & Rutley;
78, 79 *Architects' Journal*; 82 Eric de Maré;
83 Denys Lasdun & Partners; 86 Arup
Associates; 87 Eric de Maré; 89 Ralph Erskine;
90 Dennis Gilbert; 93 *Architects' Journal*;
95 James Stirling, Michael Wilford & Associates;
97 A. F. Kersting; 100 Alison and Peter Smithson.

*Part of the Eric de Maré Archive is held at the Architectural Association.

INDEX

Appropriate Technololgy 48, 50

Arup Associates 39, 86 — Prestigious London practice of architects, engineers and quantity surveyors.

Aslin, Charles Herbert 45 — 1893-1959. Hertfordshire County Architect 1945-58, President RIBA 1954-8.

Broadgate 81 — New financial centre by Liverpool Street Station, London, creating a network of streets and spaces for a wide range of activities. Architects: Skidmore, Owings and Merrill.

Brunel, Isambard Kingdom 51 — 1806-59. Engineer, designer of Clifton Suspension bridge, the steamship Great Britain.

Bullock, Alan 77 — b.1914. Master of St Catherine's College, Oxford 1960-80, Vice-Chancellor of Oxford University 1960-73. Created Baron 1976.

Burlington 97 — 1694-1753. Richard Boyle, 3rd Earl of Burlington.

Candela, Felix 64 — b.1910. Spain. After the Civil War emigrated to Mexico. 1961 awarded Auguste Perret prize by International Union of Architects. 1963 Gold Medal of Mexican Institute of Architects.

St Catherine's College 77-9 — An Oxford College founded in the 1950s. Architect: Arne Jacobsen.

Classicism 88

Le Corbusier 32, 38, 54, 76, 88 — 1887-1965. b. Charles Edouard Jeanneret, in Switzerland. 1917-65 lived and worked in Paris as painter, architect, town planner and journalist to become the most influential architect and writer on architecture in the western world. Key buildings: l'Unité d'Habitation, Marseilles; Notre Dame du Haut, Ronchamp; Le Couvent de la Sainte Marie de la Tourette; The High Court, Chandigarh, India.

Costs 30, 31

Erskine, Ralph 89 — b. 1914. English architect who based his practice in Stockholm.

Farrell, Terence 88 — b. 1938. After early partnership with Nicholas Grimshaw, moved towards Post Modernism in the 1980s, sometimes retaining a characteristic austerity, sometimes, as in MI5's building, not.

Financial Times Printing House 56 — Architect: Nicholas Grimshaw.

Foster, Norman 28, 54, 55, 68, 90 — b.1938. Early Foster Associates' buildings: Reliance Controls; Fred Olsen Amenity Centre and Passenger Terminal. The Willis, Faber & Dumas headquarters, 1975, established their reputation. 1978 Sainsbury Centre, University of East Anglia; 1979 HongKong & Shanghai Bank. Knighted 1990.

Fuller, Buckminster 73 — 1895-1983. The self-styled 'itinerant, experimental design-scientist' believed that industrialization offered the means to house 'all the people around the world', and that the primary duty of architects was to design cheap, lightweight dwellings for mass production and distribution. Also, that the care devoted to the design of 'weaponry' should be transferred, using the same resources, to the design of 'livingry'.

von Gerkan 5 — Partner in the Hamburg firm von Gerkan and Marg, architects of Stuttgart Airport.

Grimshaw, Nicholas 56 — b. 1939. From a first partnership with Farrell, Grimshaw has consistently developed an architecture whose delight is in the fixings and junctions. 1958 Oxford Ice Rink; 1988 Financial Times Printing House; 1989 Sainsbury's, Camden Town, and terrace housing; 1993 Channel Tunnel Terminus, Waterloo.

Hardwick Hall, Derbyshire 75

Hertfordshire Schools Programme 45

HongKong & Shanghai Bank 66, 68 — Architects: Norman Foster Associates.

Jacobsen, Arne 77-9 — 1902-77. Jacobsen produced fine architecture with an exceptionally small team.

Jones, Owen 51 — 1809-74. British architect who worked on the theory of colour and ornament as well as the practice.

Kahn, Louis 29, 60, 88 — 1901-74. b. Estonia. Emigrated to USA 1905. Educated in Philadelphia, where he worked in public and private offices and from 1937 ran his own practice. His buildings, their influence and that of his teaching are world wide.

Labrouste, Henri 11 — 1801-75. French architect of the Bibliothèque Nationale.

Leverton, Thomas 42 — 1743-1824. Worked on the design of Bedford Square.

Lloyd's of London 60, 61 — Architects: Richard Rogers Partnership.

Mies van der Rohe 62 — 1886-1969. Worked in Peter Behrens' Berlin office concurrently with Gropius and Le Corbusier. As Director of the Bauhaus in Hitler's time, Mies took the decision to close the school. Emigrated to USA, became Director of Illinois Institute of Technology, and continued to develop his classic steel and glass architecture of 'less is more', as at the Lake Shore Drive towers, MIT campus and Seagram.

Moro, Peter 33

Modern Movement 56, 96
Neo Classicists 88
Neo Rationalists 88
Neutra, Richard 34

Planning 63, 68, 69
Post Modern 1, 88
Pritchard, John Craven 81

Pugin, Augustus Welby 57

Quarmby, Arthur 31

RIBA 77
Richards Medical Centre, Pa. 58
Ruskin, John 57

Saarinen, Eero 85

Scale 52–4

b. Heidelberg 1911. Emigrated to England 1936. Worked with Leslie Martin on Royal Festival Hall. Became a distinguished theatre designer: eg. The Nottingham Playhouse and Theatre Royal, Plymouth.

1892–1970. An Austrian, educated in Vienna, Neutra emigrated to USA in 1923. A pillar of the Modern Movement, he was honoured in many countries.

1899–1991. Pritchard became part of the Modern Movement as a young man when he commissioned Wells Coates to build his house. This took the form of the Isokon Flats, with Pritchard's penthouse on top and the Isobar and restaurant below. Isokon Furniture, which encouraged sheet plywood to find its own form, came later. Marcel Breuer and Moholy-Nagy designed for it, as refugees from Germany, and Gropius found a haven there.
1812–52. An artist trained as architect in his father's office, Pugin based his practice on Christian beliefs. He worked with Charles Barry designing the Houses of Parliament. He wrote on the link between the quality of a society and its architecture.
An architect who explores the possibilities of plastics and pneumatic structures. He built Underhill, an underground house in W. Yorkshire, 1957.
The Royal Institute of British Architects.
Architect: Louis Kahn.
1819–1900. Artist, writer and social reformer, whose ideas on architecture were widely read, respected and followed in his lifetime, and still interest those who read them.
1910–61. Son of Finnish architect Eliel Saarinen, and partner until Fliel died. Eero Saarinen & Associates built the Trans World Airline Terminal, Idlewild, NY; Yale Ice Hockey Rink; Lincoln Center Theater; Dulles Airport Terminal, Washington DC.

Schumacher, Ernst Friedrich 48–50

Skidmore Owings and Merrill 81

Sinan, Koca 25, 93

Smithson, Alison and Peter 100

Stirling, James 95

Taylor, Sir Robert 75
Time 30
Vitruvius, Marcus 9

Wejchert, A. & D. 36

Willis, Faber & Dumas 18, 19, 20

Wilkins, William 66

Wotton, Sir Henry 9, 84, 94

Wyatt, James 75

1911–77. As Technical Advisor to third-world countries, Schumacher noticed that aid given in the form of advanced technologies often failed to take root. In looking for solutions to this problem he established the Institute of Intermediate Technology.
Architects Skidmore and Owings set up a practice in Chicago 1935, to be joined by engineer Merrill. Not only could they spot design talent but they recognized the need to support design against other professional pressures. Lever House, NY, brought them the fame they deserved and their international practice has prospered.
c. 1490–1588. Suleyman discovered Sinan in his army and appointed him architect. This proved an important discovery for architecture.
Alison 1928–93, Peter b. 1923. Established their practice 1950. The combination of intellect, sensitivity and gritty realism, highly valued by the architectural profession has, like Le Corbusier's, been under used. Their most prestigious work is The Economist group of buildings.
1926–93. Stirling had the rare gift of originality. He also demonstrated the appropriateness of external glazing to the British climate.
Early work: flats at Ham Common; History Faculty Library, Cambridge; Engineering Building, Leicester. Stirling, Wilford & Associates: Clore Galleries, Tate extension; Neue Staatsgalerie, Stuttgart.

Engineer and architect in the first century BC. His ten-volume treatise *De architectura* is still in the architectural curriculum.
The Irish architects of Holy Trinity Church, Grangemouth, Dublin.
Firm of international insurance brokers who commissioned Sir Norman Foster to design their Ipswich headquarters.
1778–1813. Architect of the National Gallery, London.
1588–1639. Developed his architectural sensibilities in Venice, where he served as British Ambassador. In 1624 he published *The Elements of Architecture*, which contains an unsurpassed definition of the art.
1746–1813. Succeeded Sir Robert Taylor as architect of Heveningham Hall, Suffolk.